RECONSTRUCTING

FAME

RECONSTRUCTING FAME

Sport, Race, and Evolving Reputations

Edited by David C. Ogden and Joel Nathan Rosen

UNIVERSITY PRESS OF MISSISSIPPI

JACKSON

www.upress.state.ms.us

The University Press of Mississippi is a member of the Association of American University Presses.

Copyright © 2008 by University Press of Mississippi
All rights reserved
Manufactured in the United States of America

First printing 2008
∞
Library of Congress Cataloging-in-Publication Data

Reconstructing fame : sport, race, and evolving reputations / edited by David C. Ogden and Joel
Nathan Rosen.
p. cm.
Includes bibliographical references and index.
ISBN 978-1-60473-091-3 (cloth : alk. paper) 1. Racism in sports—United States—History.
2. Athletes—United States—Public opinion. 3. Public opinion—United States. I. Ogden, David C.
II. Rosen, Joel Nathan, 1961– III. Title: Sport, race, and evolving reputations.
GV706.32.R43 2008
796'.089—dc22   2008007388

British Library Cataloging-in-Publication Data available

CONTENTS

CONTENTS

PART III. THE LIVING MODELS

FOREWORD

C. RICHARD KING

In his underappreciated ethnography, *Cooperstown to Dyersville*, Charles Fruehling Springwood maps the shape and significance of collective memory at the close of the twentieth century.[1] Contrasting the National Baseball Hall of Fame and its official account of the sport's past with the transformation of the location where *Field of Dreams*[2] was filmed into a popular and ephemeral tourist attraction charged with individual recollections of the family and personal connections to the game, he examines a pervasive nostalgia projected through baseball and remembrances of it. Perhaps most importantly, he finds in these sites and in his conversations with tourists, fans, sportswriters, and administrators what Raymond Williams called a structure of feeling,[3] marked most clearly by a longing to reclaim the past and make claims on the present.

Springwood nicely details the ways in which individuals and institutions manage sport's history, reminding us that who and what is forgotten is as important as who and what is remembered. And here, he directs our attention to the moral economies and cultural politics rarely visible or discussed by sport fans, or sadly even by sport scholars. Of particular interest, Springwood clarifies the differences between enshrining legends in the National Baseball Hall of Fame and redeeming fallen and/or flawed heroes by touring the site for the filming of *Field of Dreams*, a movie that centers on the metaphysical return of Shoeless Joe Jackson of the infamous Chicago Black Sox scandal. Springwood rightly traces the emergence of this new form of baseball nostalgia to a shift in familial, sexual, and racial structures in the United States and the neo-conservative reaction to them.

Since the publication of *Cooperstown to Dyersville*, the past decade has witnessed a quickening of scholarly interest in the issues taken up by Springwood, particularly his concern with the ways in which the intersections of cultural ideologies and social structures use sport to work through contradictions, manufacture consent, and contain dissent. Significantly, during this period, athletes have emerged in the media, and among the scholars who study it, as privileged sites for the construction and deconstruction of meaning, identity, community, and history.[4] While questions of race, gender, and power rightly anchor critical engagements with the representation and reception of sport stars, less discussed have been the issues of reputation, redemption, and remembrance. In this context, the present volume is a welcome addition to sport studies precisely because it asks novel questions about familiar themes, shining fresh light on the lives and significance of well-known athletes.

Together, the collected essays offer a comparative primer on the fallen athlete and his return in twentieth-century U.S. sports, detailing the circumstances surrounding their falls from grace and their subsequent comebacks. They rightly underscore the prominence of sport, and the lives of great athletes in particular, as the epicenter of moral panics, which simultaneously reinforce prevailing social relations and dominant interpretations and inflict great damage on the character and psyche of the targeted sport stars. The contributors all highlight a simple truth: whether speaking up for the rights of players, advocating for equality, or defending human rights, the perceived transgressions of great athletes have resulted in their demonization and routinely cast them out from those who once claimed to have loved them, taking from them fan support, lucrative endorsements, and often their careers.

Significantly, from my reading, a fundamental feature of the shared abjection of the athletes discussed in the subsequent essays is race. The essays detail athletes of color who spoke out, pushed back, stepped out of their place, and took a stand against prevailing social norms. Indeed, race is working in two powerful ways: on the one hand, racialized sport stars become the targets for white resentment in a manner unthinkable for white athletes, who themselves would not think to challenge the status quo, and on the other hand, the problem too often appears to be challenging the racial contract, the forms and norms of white supremacy that give reputation and redemption their force.[5]

I do not wish to rehearse the essays comprising this collection. They speak with passion and power, displaying uniform quality despite the variations in style, approach, and subject. Whatever their differences, the essays, written in often tragic tones, all take up a central concern, which may not be readily apparent: change. Each of the authors grapple with what accounts for the shifting reputation of specific athletes once celebrated, then demonized, and finally reclaimed. In turn, they address with clarity the mutability of character, community, and collective memory.

Hopefully, this volume will prompt its readers to ask: What does redemption mean now? Redemption has deep metaphysical overtones. It describes a process of finding salvation, of being absolved of sin, of cleansing oneself. The redemption of fallen athletes, while entailing a certain ritual cleansing, has little to do with the self or sin anymore, and much more to do with other ends. Indeed, redemption now appears animated by at least three distinct forces.

First, in the wake of the civil rights movement, a period in which racism (as prejudice, discrimination, and hate) has gone from overt to covert, from acceptable and expected to evil and excluded, the return of athletes formerly demonized for their commitments to social justice is less about reclaiming the individual in question and more about making claims about oneself and society in the present. As such the process of redemption has been reversed: it is not so much about the demonized athlete, who is now coveted, but about the individual or institution that wishes to cleanse itself of any association with racism and clarify its commitment to progressive values, without either reflecting on the politics of location central to such appropriations or the persistence of racism in spite of one's love for Muhammad Ali or Bill Russell or Jim Thorpe.

Second, redemption comes from outside the fallen sport star—and is anything but divine. A simple formula appears to predict when, who, and how such reclamations can happen: the redeemed athlete must be vulnerable, no longer a threat, and yet possess a cache that exudes by turns truth, danger, and power. Muhammad Ali, the fighter once despised for his resistance to racism, state violence, and the clichés of blackness, can only crossover as a marketable, approachable, and loveable figure when (a) his critique of the system has become passé, (b) common sense dictates that racial justice has been secured, (c) his physical condition makes him frail and weak, lacking control of his faculties, (d) his presentation evokes sympathy rather than fear, and (e) his audience forgets the hostility, the oppression, and the sociohistorical context and remembers only the "cool" image.

Third, the redemption of fallen athletes, especially those once stigmatized for the commitments to racial and economic justice, makes sense only in a context in which commodification and consumption have flattened history and critical distance. The past surfaces as a set of images on a screen, for instance, when an act of defiance at the 1968 Olympics is jump cut among other key events in the struggle for black freedom or to signify the rebellious spirit of the 1960s. The cool pose of old become a cool, new marketing strategy or branding device, a means of packaging discontent, opposition, and attitude to audiences who have either forgotten or never knew the true import of what Smith and Carlos did in Mexico City. Again, redemption is a strategy that does not really save the fallen as much as it attracts the alienated and the entitled.

After reading the following essays that look back at great athletes embraced once more by adoring publics, I began looking forward, wondering about the fate of some of the athletes who have fallen from grace during my lifetime. Can Pete Rose ever be recovered by the public or Major League Baseball and granted a spot in Cooperstown? Will the reputation of Michael Vick, who as I write pleads guilty to involvement in dog fighting, ever be recuperated? Or does he face eternal abjection for his deeds off the playing field? My guess is that there is little hope for either of these athletes to redeem themselves or in a generation for them to find corporations or consumers willing to embrace renewed images of these all too human champions. These two legends, forever linked in infamy will not appear on a box of Wheaties or a U.S. postage stamp. Their fate highlights an emerging trend around the moral politics of reputation and redemption. Specifically, over the past generation, the transgressions that call into question the character of athletes are not their commitments to equality, human rights, and justice; instead, the stain on their names comes from criminal acts. Whereas the changeability of the former has afforded occasions for societal reevaluation, the latter suggested a more fixed and absolute condition. Moving from the moral and political realm to a juridical domain promises few, if any, opportunities to cleanse themselves or have others reclaim them. In an increasing criminalized society, ill repute may be a life sentence for athletes who stand at odds with U.S. society.

The merit of the present volume, then, is twofold. First, it presents new ways of understanding reputation, remembrance, and redemption as well as collective memory, celebrity, and sport, asking challenging questions that push us to rethink individual lives, social relations, and cultural ideologies. Second, it clears a space for ongoing and much needed dialogues about the articulation of sport, moral economies, and cultural politics.

Before we reach that dismal future, however, we in the present must grapple with the past and how we use and abuse it in an unequal world. Given that, *Reconstructing Fame* offers a wonderful starting point for such struggles, especially for those concerned about the politics of play and the work of culture.

NOTES

1. Charles Fruehling Springwood, *Cooperstown to Dyersville: A Geography of Baseball Nostalgia* (Boulder: Westview Press, 1996).

2. Kevin Costner and James Earl Jones. *Field of Dreams*. Directed by Phil Alden Robinson. Written by W. P. Kinsella (book) and P. A. Robinson (screenplay). Los Angeles: Universal Studios, 1989.

3. See Raymond Williams, "Film and the Dramatic Tradition" in *The Raymond Williams Reader*, ed. John Higgins (Oxford: Blackwell, 2001), 33–35.

4. Good introductions to this expanding area of sport studies include Susan Birrell and Mary McDonald, eds, *Reading Sport: Critical Essays on Power and Representation* (Boston: Northeastern University Press, 2000); David Andrews and Steven J. Jackson, eds., *Sport Stars: The Cultural Politics of Sporting Celebrity* (New York: Routledge, 2001); Patrick Miller and David K. Wiggins, eds. *Sport and the Color Line: Black Athletes and Race Relations in Twentieth Century America* (New York: Routledge, 2003); and C. Richard King, ed., *Native Athletes in Sport and Society*, (Lincoln: University of Nebraska Press. 2005).

5. Charles W. Mills, *The Racial Contract* (Ithaca: Cornell University Press, 1999).

PREFACE AND ACKNOWLEDGMENTS

As is so often the case, those of us who write tend to gravitate toward projects that are spurred on by the fact that so few things out there tell the story precisely the way we would like to tell it. Such is the case with this initial salvo of our proposed multivolume series on sport and reputation. What had begun as a succinct yet admittedly terse examination of a trend toward lionizing baseball's Jackie Robinson has indeed turned into this, the first component of a project with the potential to be much more imposing yet much more comprehensive in its scope than either of us could have imagined, but one that thus far has been well received and certainly, if we can believe the tidings of others, long overdue.

The origins of this project stem from a chance encounter that began with a rather innocuous discussion in the A. Bartlett Giamatti Library facility at the National Baseball Hall of Fame and Museum in Cooperstown, New York, in June 2005. We had both come from very different sectors of the country to deliver virtually unrelated papers at the annual *Cooperstown Symposium on Baseball and American Culture*, a great place for academically inclined baseball aficionados to see what other similarly minded folks are doing in their respective fields. Regardless of the why, however, what soon evolved from this passing and certainly casual meet and greet over a cup of coffee and a handful of mini-muffins in the reception area quickly turned out to be something that both of us quickly realized had enormous potential. Dr. Ogden's vast knowledge of all things Pirate-related, and most specifically his engagement with the Roberto Clemente saga, meshed remarkably well with Dr. Rosen's appraisal of the more recent trends in the treatment of Jackie Robinson's vast cultural legacy. Before long we had sketched out a simple albeit embryonic table of contents for an initial exploration of these trends and just as effortlessly hammered out a list of future individuals and/or themes—i.e. female athletes, athletes who operate outside the American sporting landscape as well as more contemporary figures whose reputations have yet to fully play out in the public's eye—that we would like to explore in a similar fashion. From there we realized that the key to all this was to move away from a work that was strictly done on our own terms toward a much more democratic direction that employed a veritable chorus of scholars and experts at the tops of their respective games.

In terms of this particular volume, the most basic aim of this work involved us all looking at each of the individuals profiled, men of color who were chosen specifically for the way each impacted their own individual sports and, as a result, the culture at-large while we asked the seemingly elementary question "why now?" Specifically, we wanted to know why each athlete, this far beyond that individual's playing career, had been discovered or at the very least rediscovered within a more modern context.

Now on the surface this might appear to be a rather matter-of-fact and perhaps even easily dismissed query, but, and as the reader will note throughout the course of this compilation, it is a much more taxing question once one starts winding down that path. Most notable in these critiques is how the reputation-related matters addressed become particularly problematic when mixed with the baggage inherent to color, the tie that certainly binds these subjects together. The very fact that both Robinson and Clemente, as well as Flood and Russell and, really, everyone else whose upward trajectory is chronicled herein, have found themselves near or at the center of many of the more modern discussions of sport is certainly noteworthy, if not remarkable. As a consequence, as we began to investigate the possibilities inherent to such a study, it became readily apparent that this is indeed a tale yet to be told, an intriguing narrative that takes into account the way that sport, color, reputation, culture, national memory, and nostalgia are separately and in a bloc most deserving of a very proper and very public airing.

The authors whose works are before you consist of a diverse, accomplished, and self-consciously multidisciplinary group traversing seven separate and distinct fields of inquiry who bring great expertise and passion to their individual subjects. Their work on this project has been exemplary as demonstrated best by their ability to move beyond mere biography in order to probe more deeply into those very matters we sought to raise in our own contributions, which we believe will ultimately endow this effort and any subsequent ventures with its own particular place among the literature. Bringing such a group together was a real *coup* for us, and we hope that they realize how fortunate we know we are to have found them.

The editors would like to offer our appreciation to a number of people whose contributions to this work were of inestimable value. First of all, to all the contributors who have stuck with this from the start, you are the backbone of this endeavor, and our gratitude for your graciousness, earnestness, and faithfulness is immeasurable.

To Craig Gill and Valerie Jones at the University Press of Mississippi, your abilities to work in, around, through, and beside our vision was extraordinary. More importantly, your encouragement and professional direction gave us those lifts when we needed them most.

Individually, Dr. Rosen would like to thank Mark S. Gutentag, Karen Kilps, Tanya Gable, Drs. Daniel Jasper and Bettie Smolansky, Monte Irvin, and Jerry Weissman for their material as well as their intellectual inspiration while Dr. Ogden would like to thank Connie, David, Jr. and Rachel for their lifelong patience and Drs. Hugh Cowdin and Robert Carlson for their initial encouragement in developing a baseball research agenda.

Thanks as well to MaryKay Waite-Rosen for her invaluable clerical assistance.

David C. Ogden and Joel Nathan Rosen, Editors

INTRODUCTION

Examining Reputations within a Cultural Context

DAVID C. OGDEN AND JOEL NATHAN ROSEN

INTRODUCTION

Dating back to earliest developments in both oral and written traditions, the concept of the reputation has served as a useful tool in terms of defining the natures and conditions of a given order by serving as a core around which history is created. Consciously or otherwise, societies and cultures have long used reputations to construct their own cherished myths and legends. As sociologist Gary Alan Fine, whose own reputation in this field is virtually unmatched, has argued, reputations define the boundaries of society, flagging the fringes while demarcating evil as well as excellence.[1]

Still, while reputations are the standards against which others are judged, they are seldom stable. The advent and proliferation of communication technologies and systems have provided tribunals for the introduction of new information and the questioning of old information relative to persons of cultural, social, or historic interest. Additionally, and as the work of several scholars has suggested, they are often underscored by various forays into national and/or cultural memory and are highly susceptible to nostalgic twists and turns.[2]

In his lengthy treatise on cultural memory and the propensity for uncritical and certainly even destructive bouts of cultural revisionism, historian David Lowenthal observes that the outcome, intended or otherwise, of attempts to reposition misinterpreted or otherwise miscalculated reputations through what often becomes a counterintuitive attempt to highlight past transgressions inevitably leads to an exaggerated presentation of such matters. He notes: "The past is always altered for motives that reflect present needs. We reshape our heritage to make it attractive in modern terms; we seek to make it part of ourselves, and ourselves part of it; we conform it to our self-images and aspirations. Rendered grand or homely, magnified or tarnished, history is continually altered in our private interests or on behalf of our community or country."[3] Or as Füredi contends, an idealized history "tries to recover a shared past to help forge a common identity. It uses the mask of the past to mobilize society for some purpose in the present."[4] In this regard, reputations when viewed outside their unique social or cultural context are inherently problematic and certainly in need of a tighter degree of scrutiny and investigation.

ATHLETIC REPUTATIONS

Given their ubiquitousness within cultural spaces, sports figures have long served as ample subjects for such public discussions. Indeed, as societies and cultures change, so too do reputations and how those reputations were initially cast in their historical and cultural contexts.

National and international events, the agenda set by mass media and news organizations, and the flux of public opinion can cast the public image of well-known individuals into different molds, and recent events in American life certainly underscore this case in point. Media consumers are well aware of the row that ensued in 2003 when members of The Dixie Chicks, the folk-inspired Country and Western band, openly condemned the actions of President George W. Bush and the United States in its pursuit and conduct of the war in Iraq. The resulting fall-out, engineered as it was by private interests operating in public spaces, led to the band's temporary out-casting, though as times changed and the administration and its actions became subject to even more critical challenges, so too would the band's reputation receive a notable jolt back into public favor.

Certainly this was by no means the first time that such an entity was to suffer a setback because of actions or comments deemed to run afoul of the social mores of an era. Nor would these women be the first nor the last to find themselves caught in the sort of flux that would take them from acclaim to disrepute back to acclaim in a relatively short period of time. What this example demonstrates, however, is that these events can often be orchestrated from both within as well as outside the public eye, and conscious or not, these sorts of actions can serve as powerful markers for determining who stands inside and outside public favor.

Historic figures in sport, such as the men profiled in this particular text, have undergone a similar degree of flux as administered through the efforts of media outlets in parallel with the explosion of data available in this particularly information-driven age. But unlike the speed with which we see The Chicks fall out and back in favor, the reputations of these men represent a much more insidious version of the modern seeming path to glory, and at a rather staggering cost. The increasingly recognized notion that the media can both reflect the times and as well as shape them serves in this regard to amplify the notion that reputations can be made, broken, revisited, and subsequently deconstructed again in a virtual blink of the eye, but the speed with which these changes occur often times belies a much more problematic nature of such events while at the same time leaving a set of engineered and often impossible set of standards that future generations are often unprepared to reconcile in their context.

A media-induced reputation, which is more typically how such constructions come about, can over a longer period reshape and redefine the image and legacy of cherished icons while providing a novel but often troubling baseline for behavior and behavioral standards for those operating in the present. Print medium, such as the nation's top-selling sport-inspired magazines or even the sports pages of the ubiquitous daily press, for example, remind readers of past feats and accomplishments but always in a modern context filled with self-flattery and preconceived assumptions. Similarly, electronic outlets such as the ESPN Classic cable-TV network that profiles and unabashedly celebrates past sports icons or HBO Sports with its propensity for grandiloquent documentary reinforces both cultural and social stature but again often against the backdrop of modernity while virtually sneering at contemporary figures who for the most part are guilty of nothing more than lacking the same degree of temporal or spatial separation as those profiled.

Such attempts by press and media, social organizations and collectives, and other forms and fora of public discourse to commemorate any given sport legend can indeed result in shifts in popular perceptions that often serve to obfuscate rather than enhance an actor's role in sport history while serving to rewrite sizeable portions of historical context as a means to manipulate the very image of the present itself. Moreover, this slapdash treatment of social and cultural narratives not only lacks coherence but also serves to trivialize the efforts of some of sport's more significant figures and those associated with them, while at the same time presents virtually unattainable social markers for everything from achievement to deportment for those who operate in the here and now.

Where such models enter into the lexicon of a given order seems to reside within the notion that people use these sorts of preconceived models, or heuristics, to categorize or characterize individuals and their behavior. Moreover, such characterizations are often formed within a social frame that tends to be obscured by a host of socially governed rationales, many of which are nonetheless problematic in their own right. As Fine contends, a reputation consists of "a socially recognized persona: an organizing principle by which the actions of a person . . .can be linked together."[5] Adding color to this mix, as we do herein, takes an already precarious matter, one filled with supposition and the weight of age-old cultural baggage, and further muddies up attempts to sort through the resulting construction and reconstruction of each contributor's place within the culture itself.

THE REDEMPTION OF MUHAMMAD ALI

The trajectory of the life and career of former heavyweight champion Muhammad Ali (who was consciously omitted from this volume for a host of reasons, not the least of which is that his story has been explored already in countless forms) serves as an excellent model for the discussion brought forth herein. A former Olympic champion stripped of the chance to defend his world heavyweight title because of his politics, Ali became the target of criticism by other sports figures, government officials, media, and all measure of national leaders alike. Years would pass before he was allowed to once again ply his trade in the ring, and decades would pass before he would regain a portion of the iconic status that he had once enjoyed from an adoring American public.

The dramatic change in the way Americans have come to regard Ali today, however, is little short of astonishing, though it is nonetheless genuine. Whereas he was once acclaimed as one of the most controversial—if not divisive—figures in America, both in the ring and outside of it, he has come to be heralded as a sort of deity in decades well beyond his prime for reasons that often seem to offer neither consistency nor rationality. Here was a man who in his physical prime was imposing, overtly self-confident, and certainly unprecedented in the emergent media age. He could most easily be viewed as a potentially dangerous admixture of former heavyweight champ Jack Johnson and a less subtle but no less problematic Malcolm X, though to be sure it was his prowess in the ring alongside that infectious personality that garnered him such acclaim while affording him a certain degree of exception to the rules that once governed the behavior of African American men.

The nation, already in the throes of an extraordinary fragmentation during an era of challenges ranging from the war in Viet Nam to the ongoing struggle for civil rights, indeed saw Ali in a very mixed light. For some he embodied the essence of black power and black pride, and his well-publicized conversion to Islam and his frequent and equally well-publicized meetings with Malcolm X, Elijah Muhammad, and other so-deemed black radicals of the day, including several of the men profiled herein, left even some of the most liberalized elements in America wondering. Moreover, in positions of power and prominence, Ali's continued presence and soaring popularity, if only in the ring, made his presence uniquely problematic. Thus, the ensuing turn of events that would dramatically alter his life then, while perhaps predictable, given what we now know about the age, was exceedingly calculated even during the height of an age in which on-going surveillance projects such as COINTEL were in place to keep radical elements from further encroaching into the mainstream of American life. Thus, Ali's very decisive and highly publicized fall from public favor, resulting ostensibly from his refusal to be inducted into the U.S. military and his subsequent fight for both his freedom and the return of his boxing credentials, is much more easily viewed through the context of that particular time frame.

For the American establishment in dire need of a strategic victory, Ali would seem to represent the quintessential victory, and something to which a majority of Americans appeared willing to accept on its face. It would not be until well after his career was over and the emergence of a new chapter in Ali's life that a more public outcry regarding what many believe today to have been the systemic violation of Ali's civil liberties turned Ali from a sort of villainous character to a more sympathetic hero for the age. In this regard, the construction of Ali much later in his life was shaped less by an awareness of what was then the contemporary tide of circumstances that led to his public fall and more so by an almost nostalgic reinterpretation of yesterday against the backdrop of the present.

To be sure, a twenty-first-century Ali is a different matter altogether. Stripped of his dignity and his imposing physical presence and ravaged by a debilitating neurological disorder, he has found a receptive populace once denied him during his prime. Moreover, now damaged and well beyond the capacity to fight—both in the ring and out of it—he has nevertheless gained an acceptance and an entirely new set of behavioral conceits that seem remarkably removed from an age in which he could actually stand proudly and speak for himself. In essence, he has become, for lack of a better definition, the perfect embodiment of a heroic icon in an age that simply cannot conceptualize, let alone tolerate the notion that a hero can set his or her own agenda. Thus, a shaking and debilitated Ali, whose new reputation was essentially forged as a result of his appearance at the 1996 Summer Olympic Games in Atlanta, has become in every sense both a literal as well as a figurative torchbearer for the age: a tragic and deeply flawed yet evocative figure whom even the most ardent detractors can now support while washing their hands of complicity in what had occurred prior. Furthermore, Ali's redemption by something not of his own doing underscores a much more complex and problematic design, contemporary in its scope, for how celebrity is formed, recognized, and tolerated in an age that at best seems shaken by the notion of celebrity while at the same time unable or perhaps simply unwilling to ignore it. Namely, if this is to be the contemporary shape of redemption, what then becomes the point of redemption at all?

THE PROJECT

The processes and paths by which vilification becomes redemption marks the focus of this particular collection of essays. In every case, the reputation of each personality featured went through a similar set of circumstances in terms of a striking general reappraisal of his character while enduring in one form or another an equally striking and steadily imposed form of revision that continues to underscore the more consumption-friendly ethos (some might counter *pathos*) of the age.

Paying particular attention to male twentieth-century sport icons whose skin color was a key consideration in the early evaluations of their careers by the public and the press, we feature herein the efforts and scholarship of intellectuals from a wide range of theoretical disciplines who offer an even wider range of explanations of how select social agents and institutions construct and deconstruct the narratives surrounding these select figures. Throughout, each contributor has attempted to disentangle the various myths that have come to mark the popular conceptions of each subject, subjects who were chosen specifically for their contributions to various debates regarding the role and image of the American athlete and to reposition and clarify their places as twentieth-century icons beyond the mythology of color, sport, achievement, and celebrity. These subjects were chosen not just for their athletic and cultural prowess, but also for the reputational cycles that their careers represent and that can be found in today's athletes who occupy similar spaces of notoriety. What we have found in this regard, and to paraphrase Prosper Godonoo in his brilliant piece on Paul Robeson here, is that in the end, the more interesting tale is the one woven from the demythologized fabric rather than the calculated fiction! Thus, it is through events, social upheavals, and a seemingly endless array of cultural changes and exchanges, that the reputations of each of these men, once formed and subsequently recast in a remarkably innovative light, demonstrate clearly the fragility of the lines that separate the so-called *good* from the so-called *bad* reputations and the ramifications found within the constructions of each.

The methods used to explore the evolution of what we, the editors, have taken to considering *once-tainted* reputations are marked by a range of theoretical constructs and discipline-specific approaches that underscore the editors' overarching desire to preserve the interdisciplinary nature of this study. Moreover, the flow of the book is organized in such a way as to offer a wealth of parallel and contrasting elements that tend to accentuate as well as compliment each successive effort, which is what accounts for each distinctive albeit specific section headings.

Appearing in the initial section, for example, David C. Ogden, in his chapter on Roberto Clemente and the speed with which Clemente's reputation enjoyed a virtual overnight redemption as a result of his untimely death, attempts to explain this rather abrupt departure through the prism of dual process theories, specifically the continuum model of impression formation. Employing the work of Fiske et al,[6] Ogden demonstrates that while there are several models with which to explain how impressions of an individual can be formed by another in a remarkably short time frame, he further contends that it can also be applied to studying collective impressions. That is, the impressions that many people hold of one person and how those impressions are formed over long periods of time demonstrate tremendous potential for expanding our understanding of both how reputations change and what changing suggests. Moreover, by contending that reputations are based, at least in part, on impression formation, Ogden's reasoning follows that of Fine and others who have looked at these questions in terms of both constructionist theory as well as others who have attempted to explain cultural memory and the resiliency of national narratives.[7]

The case of Roberto Clemente, one of the two archetypical figures featured in this opening segment of the text, helps us further examine the parallels between impression and reputation formation and discuss the social agents involved in that formation. More specifically, as Ogden elaborates, press and media are among those social agents and, through their power to set the public agenda, are key players in reputation formation, a trend that seems to work just as easily for Clemente as for the other subjects tackled throughout the text.

Joel Nathan Rosen's more outwardly polemical approach to the matter of Jackie Robinson's early twenty-first-century reputation serves as a counterpoint to Ogden's more theoretically driven contribution. Rosen concedes that while Robinson, like Clemente, is enjoying a remarkable as well as posthumous embrace, the cost is often obscured by the false and often disingenuous promotion of racial tolerance and acceptance through the Robinson saga. Rosen argues that rather than view the more ubiquitous characterizations of Robinson as indicative as a triumph of democracy and progress, the Robinson mystique should be viewed as being too often trivialized by virtue of its continued trumpeting of duty and comportment that belie the range of complex premises that lay beneath the unabashed cheerleading. Thus, rather than presuming that the trend toward lionizing Robinson as a folk hero stands poised to dim or even blur the color line, Rosen contends that what simmers in spite of the openly revisionist tone is a discourse that in fact mutes the notion of racial justice while rendering it banal.

The second section of the text, one that was intended to highlight those revamped legacies that are either buried under the weight of a seeming glut of celebrity or simply forgotten by a population bombarded by similar tales of less-daunting characters, begins with David L. Leonard's brilliant retrospective of the life and legacy of Curt Flood. Placed firmly outside the tired mythology of martyred fugitive or tragic fall guy that so typically follows the Flood legacy, Leonard's portrayal of Flood comes from deep within the dual centers of the often poorly articulated link between skin color and class. This, above all else, adds a remarkable degree of substance to what has become a rather moribund cautionary tale that often comes replete with Flood's trials rather than his successes and his personal indiscretions as opposed to his classically heroic composition.

Stepping away from the more modern inspiration of Flood, Prosper Godonoo offers a most poignant and lyrical reminder of the many ways that Paul Robeson embodied the American ideal without ever being afforded such a luxury in his own lifetime. Fêted by today's standards, Robeson's reputation may indeed epitomize Fine's conceptualization of the "difficult reputation,"[8] especially when one stops to consider the ramifications of a black man, gifted physically and intellectually and comprising a skill-set virtually unequaled in his time, who became a virtual pariah in his own country for having the audacity to say the things that needed to be said that few in his position would. Equally as compelling is the way in which Godonoo can depict that same figure who has today been conveniently resurrected to serve as the beacon of comportment as a means to quell, if not outright retard, the visions of those who today occupy a similar space but are presumed unable to measure up to a standard that only reached iconic status long after the subject was both discredited and safely put back in his place.

Robert W. Reising's musings on the legacy of Jim Thorpe too speak to this point in several unique ways. In spite of the fact that Thorpe is the only Native addressed specifically in this collection, he might very well be its most tragic. As Reising poses him, Thorpe was consciously developed to be a uniquely physical being, but though he would become exactly as his handlers had anticipated, he is subsequently betrayed by the very same faction that helped construct both his athletic prowess and his burgeoning reputation. Moreover, and similarly to Robeson, Thorpe embodied all those elements of physical brilliance as espoused in those vaunted American myths regarding masculine deportment and grace as espoused in the affected novels of Gilbert Patton, aka Burt L. Standish, creator of those extraordinarily impacting Frank Merriwell stories, and the serials featuring the quintessential American youth that was Jack Armstrong,[9] but with one glaring exception: while Thorpe could play the role of the All-American boy, he could never look like the part no matter how many medals, records, and international endorsements he could muster.

As Reising so eloquently observes, "America's script called for a Caucasian of Anglo ancestry to be the sports hero of the land." Destroyed, thus, by prejudice and exploitation both, Thorpe too has been resurrected to serve as a sort of ghost of an athletic past that never really existed but stands nonetheless as an unattainable obstacle for the modern athlete who might similarly find himself running along the periphery.

The last section of the book is devoted to the living symbols of this move toward redemption that often reads as a parody of their lives and accomplishments. What separates these subjects from the others already noted is that their reputations have yet to be fully cemented into the culture, leaving some aspects of their redemption to remain as-of-yet reconstructed.

Murry Nelson's reflections on a freshly minted and made-for-the-twenty-first-century Bill Russell chronicles the rise of a man who until recently could never have been mistaken for the same gentle giant who seems to cascade ubiquitously across American television screens and sports pages. As Nelson recounts, Russell's reputation was built on the complex and certainly contradictory footing that so often surrounded accomplished men of color in the public eye who were exceptionally gifted and driven both. Russell at any one time could be surly, unapproachable, outspoken, and even self-admittedly militant. He was also the winningest athlete of the modern era, which both endeared and disconnected him from the very fan-base that sought to embrace him, though always from afar and in the context of the next championship. A post-career Russell, however, becomes something of a caricature of himself but only, as Nelson suggests, because no one bothered to attempt to get to know the man in the first place. His infectious laugh combined with the footage of a fierce competitor plying his trade has today made him something of an anomaly—a once publicly tainted celebrity afforded the opportunity to rewrite his own legacy for a more modern age but always under the watchful eye of others. And as if to fully underscore this development, Russell, who once eschewed the spotlight, has today embraced it as an ambassador of goodwill and a paradigm of comportment and virtue that oddly upholds many of the same obstacles to liberty that he once attacked in his youth.

A similar sense of confusion exists in the more modern reappraisal of the reputations of Tommie Smith and John Carlos. Forever linked by a fleeting yet powerful moment, theirs is perhaps the most challenging of all the legacies herein and primarily because the nation as a whole has yet to fully come to terms with the nature of the act that both conjoined them to one another while separating them as individuals from the public at large.

As author Urla Hill explains, the challenge of attempting to place Smith and Carlos in any sort of context is informed solely by the perception of what took place in Mexico City and why. Yet, in spite of myriad books, articles, debates, and even documentaries, there remains such a wide range of conjecture and assumptions that continue to swirl about each man's role in what has been popularly deemed "a black power protest" that trying to move beyond 1968 often proves to be futile. Thus, as with Russell, though certainly in a much more pronounced fashion, theirs is a legacy not even close to being written, though perhaps the most glaring aspect of this is that the very conditions that originally prompted their history-making moment continue to take a backseat to it all.

A NOTE ON REDEMPTION

The idea that we have self-consciously sought to utilize the grandiloquent notion of *redemption* is to be viewed here both in terms of its authenticity as well as its ironic possibilities. The fact is that while each of these subjects has undergone some sort of rehabilitation through the years, whether or not they have actually been redeemed, or whether or not redemption can actually be possible (or even plausible) in a material sense, or whether or not any of these men have ever even sought redemption is a teleological matter for philosophers and psychologists alike to ponder and is certainly well beyond the scope of this work. Still, its continued presence around the nucleus of each subject does indeed offer some substantive, if not spirited, points to consider.

The reader should also note that while these essays depend heavily on some form of narrative that often intersects with biography, they are not meant to be simply a re-telling of events and career highlights but rather a means to explore these individuals much more completely. As Boym reminds, "Nostalgia is about the relationship between individual biography and the biography of groups or nations, between personal and collective memory."[10]

Thus, and as mentioned previously, the aim of this volume is to rummage about the various discussions of these individuals while dredging up some of the more subtle and otherwise nuanced observations that mark the process and processes by which their reputations have developed, evolved, and ultimately expanded. In this regard, and solely in terms of the theme at hand, the figures who appear in this volume are to be thought of as vehicles for exploring these broadly defined themes and as new standards by which reputations-in-the-making can be evaluated and tracked long-term. Through all of their collective accomplishments and struggles, these celebrated subjects have themselves contributed powerfully, if not hauntingly, to the development of the nation's social, cultural, and political armories.

NOTES

1. Gary Alan Fine, *Difficult Reputations: Collective Memories of the Evil, Inept, and Controversial* (Chicago: The University of Chicago Press, 2001), 4.

2. See, for example, Barry Schwartz, "The Social Context of Commemoration: A Study in Collective Memory," *Social Forces* 6, no. 12 (December 1982): 374–402; Frank Füredi, *Mythical Past, Elusive Future: History and Society in an Anxious Age* (London: Pluto Press, 1992); Frank Füredi, *Where Have All the Intellectuals Gone? Confronting 21st Century Philistinism* (London: Continuum, 2004); and Svetlana Boym, *The Future of Nostalgia* (New York: Basic Books, 2001).

3. David Lowenthal, *The Past Is a Foreign Country* (Cambridge, UK: Cambridge University Press, 1988), 348.

4. Füredi, *Mythical Past, Elusive Future*, 62.

5. Fine, *Difficult Reputations*, 2.

6. Susan T. Fiske, Miao-Hsiang Lin, and Steven L. Neuberg, "The Continuum Model: Ten Years Later," in *Dual-Process Theories in Social Psychology*, eds. Shelly Chaiken and Yaacov Trope (New York, NY: The Guilford Press, 1999), 231–54.

7. Fine, *Difficult Reputations*.

8. Fine, *Difficult Reputations*.

9. See, for example, Gilbert Patton aka Burt L. Standish. *Frank Merriwell at Yale*. (Charleston, SC: BiblioBazaar, 2006).

10. Boym, *The Future of Nostalgia*, xvi.

PART I

THE
ARCHETYPES

CONSTRUCTING BANALITY

The Trivialization of the Jackie Robinson Legacy

JOEL NATHAN ROSEN

Did you see Jackie Robinson hit that ball?
Did he hit it? Yeah, but that ain't all . . .
—The Count Basie Orchestra, 1949[1]

INTRODUCTION

In the days leading up to the fiftieth anniversary of Jackie Robinson's breaking the colorline in baseball in 1947, veteran Major League Baseball star (and conceivably borderline Hall-of-Fame candidate) Frank Thomas was asked if he ever pondered Jackie Robinson's role in setting the stage for modern American sport. To the bewilderment (read: disgust) of many, Thomas responded almost stoically, "Not really. I'm really more about the New Age."[2]

As difficult as it is to imagine, given the atmosphere surrounding the approach of this much-heralded milestone, and whatever Thomas meant when he referred to himself as a product of a so-called *new age*, his lack of reverence regarding the Jackie Robinson legacy also spoke to the fear of power brokers as well as the keepers of the nation's ethical canons who have freely been able to parcel the Robinson saga as part of a much larger repository for well-cherished moral principles. Indeed, the significance of Robinson's breaking down vestiges of what were then conventional racial barriers, the timing of his struggle, and the level of personal sacrifice he displayed throughout his time in Major League Baseball, as well as in his many post-career undertakings, cannot be so easily dismissed, but whenever these sorts of clashes occur, whenever a younger generation seems determined to turn its collective back on its elders, the results often lead to the more mordant speculation that somehow youth just does not get it.

Now whether Thomas's lack of engagement with Robinson and his struggles can be extrapolated to encompass the modern athlete as a whole may be entirely beside the point, though there is every indication that this may indeed be the case. Still, what is the more pressing point is that for those who contend that sport should stand for

3

something more than mere athletic excellence, the Jackie Robinson story can most certainly be construed as the embodiment of such claims. In the case of a figure as celebrated and virtually sacrosanct as Robinson, Thomas's seeming inability or perhaps even refusal to live and breathe his struggle can in some corners be interpreted as the epitome of heresy while lending further credence to a cynical and increasingly popular assumption that the modern athlete is neither a worthy recipient of public adulation nor appreciative enough to be afforded the trappings of celebrity.

PERPETUATING AN ICON

Without a doubt, for those of us of a certain age, Robinson has been (and remains) a poignant and heroic figure, one who has been presented in countless retellings of the narrative, some of which have been leftover from our childhood memories while others were brought to us in a much more erudite fashion. Nevertheless, and regardless of presentation, it has long been apparent that his was a struggle born of unfathomable hardship that certainly bears our rapt attention, which is what makes Robinson such an integral feature within the culture—an archetypical figure who in spite of the popular adoration remains cloaked in a most complex and complicated nature.

What makes so many of the more recent and even modern-seeming accounts of the Robinson story both so compelling and astonishing at the same time, and to be quite candid here, is that so many of the more recent attempts to chronicle this decidedly central narrative have proven to be not merely banal but, rather, dispiriting attempts to couch the Robinson tale in a language filled with reprimand and reproach that leaves it reflecting less the human capacity to act and to act resolutely, as so readily demonstrated by Robinson himself, and more evocative of a view of human nature that is steeped in the sort of pathos indicative of a much more widespread antipathy consisting of, among other things, anxiety, paralysis, and fear that more often than not typifies our modern age. Thus, while the marking of the anniversary was timely and certainly warranted, a more careful reading of recent portrayals of Robinson and of his place within American cultural spaces leaves the impression that Robinson's legacy, in spite of the constant retelling, remains manifestly ill- or even un-defined, making it a much more problematic notion to assess amid the cacophony of modern sport and the omnipresent clamor for a competitive paradigm that better reflects the character of twenty-first-century ideals.[3]

The fundamental elements that have come to denote the ongoing battle to define the Robinson construct often come down to a sort of binary that works through the dual assumptions that Robinson was either an exemplary figure whose fight demonstrated a far-reaching and universal aim, or that he was a tragic figure whose legend can be used to demonstrate the failure of contemporary actors to operate in a morally acceptable fashion. Between the binary, however, there exists other elements of Robinson's legacy that hold enormous sway among the populace. For example, there is the blanket assumption that Robinson's ascension to the major leagues marks no less than the foundation of the struggle to promote racial justice in American life, leaving his service to race and country well beyond reproach. Furthermore, his continued presence over both America as a whole and African America to be more specific swirl about in such a way as to incite a veritable avalanche of supposition and conjecture, leaving in its wake a series of uncritical and veritably irrelevant elements that range from the inspirational to the implausible. In this respect, modern critiques of the Robinson narrative fall tediously into the category of national myth and serve not to enhance but rather to detract from the discussion in such a way as to render it trivial and banal. But as David Lowenthal makes clear in his discussion of what he maintains is a more fashionable inclination to show cherished memories in the form of "creative anachronism,"[4] this reading of Robinson is not about Robinson per se but about us and how we see ourselves juxtaposed to the world we ourselves have constructed. Moreover, by removing Robinson from the context of his own unique historical circumstances, we run the risk of taking all meaning out of his accomplishments by assigning to them cause and effect relationships that are not grounded in an actual historical setting but, rather, one that is steeped in a nostalgic fog that offers us little beyond parable. Thus, a more modern rendering of Robinson and the way we remember the man and his achievements today may be an even more significant marker of where we are than the very notions that he has come to represent in his own unique and historical context.

As we inch closer toward the sixtieth year of Robinson's ascent into national prominence, it would appear, thus, that rather than being even more certain as to the place that Robinson occupies within the culture, we have discovered instead a much more ambiguous sense of it. It has become equally apparent that inherent to these more recent developments, there has crept into this narrative a notably uncritical air that often serves not to enhance but rather to obfuscate Robinson's role in postwar American life while leaving in its wake a plot-line that lacks coherence that at the end of the day devalues his struggle and the work of those connected to it. Therefore, one is moved to ask:

• can we hope to discover a legacy for Robinson amid the increasingly blurred depictions?
• and if so, is it possible to do so critically and within a more accurate context that both demonstrates an affective model for human activity while keeping the most fundamental elements of his legacy from straying beyond their implications?

DIFFICULT ASSUMPTIONS

There are several theoretical motifs that we can employ in our search for a more material understanding of Robinson's contributions to American life that range from the matters of national and cultural memory to the construction of what sociologist Gary Alan Fine refers to as "difficult reputations,"[5] of which the lack of coherence concerning the Robinson saga, as it were, certainly demonstrates outwardly. Fine posits that in the case of most national icons, be they lauded or reviled, the tendency for us to speculate rather than critically investigate the material significance of the celebrated leads toward what he calls the "thinness of our knowledge of [celebrity] figures."[6] Fine maintains that notable gaps in our collective interpretation of the groups and/or individuals whom we claim shape our common identity are born of a collective torpor that offers, among other things, blueprints for the building of an ineffective citizenry rather than being a matter of setting the record straight. Citing C. H. Cooley's assertion that fame is constructed around a narrative that is need-based rather than factually engineered,[7] Fine contends that the building and maintenance of national reputations allow us to assemble our world in such a way as to reflect long-established values that may or may not intersect with the more factual reading of a particular symbol's contribution. He notes: "Our chronicles, particularly those by which we instruct our young, often appear to be nothing more than linked biographies. We find it easy to think about the past by focusing on the lives of people whom we see as having created events; history becomes a personalistic narrative dripping with agency."[8]

By Fine's reckoning, this tendency for girding content toward socially affective outcomes is indicative of our particularly self-indulgent times.[9] In the case of Jackie Robinson, it allows us to reconstruct a Robinson-based narrative while conceivably rewriting controversial and even objectionable areas of our own national reputation that comes off as less critical and analytical while conveying a significant degree of revisionist content. As Fine would later admonish, "If [we] cannot be honest brokers when [we] strive to be *reputational* entrepreneurs, at least in some measure [we] should be honest analysts, different in kind from those who consciously attempt to massage history."[10]

In terms of the Robinson legend, what we seem to have before us is a trail of contradictory elements followed often by a mass of conjecture that warrants further scrutiny amidst growing ambiguity. In terms of the binary that generally serves to manage the Robinson narrative, there are those who view Robinson strictly through the prism of civil rights activism, placing his rise and subsequent flourish in Major League Baseball alongside a parade of figures who helped engineer the coming civil rights battles. While scholars are certainly prone to latch on to these types of depictions, by and large these sorts of illustrations tend to be of a more popular vein and are primarily the work of news commentators, pop-historians, and, in a more general sense, custodians of a much wider degree of national mythologies who are attempting to bring to the general population a solid mixture of editorial guile alongside a strong celebratory earnestness. In this regard, Robinson and his unique sacrifices can be demonstrated in such a manner as to point the way to a more egalitarian future that at one time was assumed to be capable of forcing a post–World

War II America to face up to the indefensible hypocrisy of fighting injustice abroad while in effect ignoring the long string of prejudice continuing to unravel at home, something, I might add, that has proven to be fallacious in just about every aspect in spite of attempts to suggest otherwise.

The flipside of this discussion rests in the reinterpretation of what appears to have been the end-result or at least the unintended consequences of Robinson's role in unraveling the vagaries of segregation in mainstream American sport. This challenge to more popularly aligned assumptions tests Robinson's role as archetypical hero. Moreover, it asserts that while the actions that led to baseball's integration were laudable, historically significant, and heroic on their collective face, the initial gains achieved by African Americans, in this particular case, through the Rickey-Robinson collaborative have also led to a general malaise, which in this case leads critics toward what can be deemed the dilemma of what some maintain is a dramatic level of sport fetishism poised to appropriate the dreams, energies, and aspirations of minority youth. If nothing else, this thread of commentary serves to lay bare the notion that what was once dubbed "baseball's great experiment"[11] marked in essence a tragic turn in the fight for lasting and genuine equality while restating the extent to which we remain unconvinced in regard to our perception of these circumstances.[12]

MEMORIES ARE MADE OF THESE

As noted in the above, the challenge of confronting the fashion with which reputations are constructed is underscored by a litany of motives that can best be captured within the duality of reminiscence and nostalgia. In the case of sport, if we are in any way to gravitate toward Clifford Geertz's by-now ubiquitous claim that sport is part of a story we tell ourselves,[13] then the method by which we narrate our own story suggests even more about how we see ourselves relative to that particular chapter of our self-narrative.

As a number of scholars have attempted to demonstrate in regard to the construction of national and cultural memory, there is an inevitable point to which we, as a collective order, end up removing the context from our most cherished memories not because we no longer see value in them but, rather, because we have begun to more vigorously search for a more transcendent sense of purpose within the context of our own life and times. This search becomes the driving mechanism behind both our thoughts and our memories, and forces us to constantly reevaluate the meanings implied or suggested that swirl about our heads that come pouring out in a concoction popularly regarded as nostalgia.[14]

In her exploration of the role of nostalgia in creating national character, for example, Harvard professor of Slavic languages and literature Svetlana Boym maintains that the more typical outcomes inherent to constructions brought to life in the formation of a national consciousness often serve to reduce the historical context to an easily traced and singularly imbued storyline, one in which the ideal rather than the exigent is virtually always the result.[15] Under these conditions, Boym contends that we leave ourselves prone to overindulgence while we seek out models from which we may rescue ourselves from the most emblematic and problematic elements of modernity. Because, she maintains, these models lack a context that is temporally unique and, are, by definition, already antiquated, we end up, as Lowenthal suggests, "[s]eeing the past in our own terms"[16] while reshaping artifacts and memories only in so much as they fit the underlying objective. In this respect, the tendency to land on the sunnier side of yesteryear serves to rewrite a past that not only never occurred as such but could never broker a more favorable arrangement for the modern world. It is, as Lowenthal sardonically casts it, reminiscent of an ideal world in which everything operated safely and efficiently that inevitably forces us to reconsider the fallacies of the present. As he puts it, in this idealized yet fictional world, "there is no dung, no puddles, no weeds."[17] In other words, a world inspired by nostalgic recollection lies, as Boym concedes, on "a utopian dimension that consists in the exploration of other potentialities and unfulfilled promises of modern happiness."[18]

A favorable reading of yesteryear, however, is but one of the many characteristics inherent to an uncritical embrace of nostalgia. Füredi, for example, concedes that when the past is constantly awash in a complimentary glow, the present becomes increasingly seen in pejorative terms. Echoing Marx's contention that history is "nothing but the activity of man pursuing his aims,"[19] Füredi counters that the extent to which nostalgia hovers about modernity removes not merely the human element from the equation but also stands tall in reminding that human activity is in and of itself the problem,[20] a condition that ultimately allows the past to lie on much more favorable and comfortable footing. As Halbwachs reveals, "No memory is possible outside frameworks used by people living in society to determine and retrieve their recollections."[21] Or as Barry Schwartz explains: "Given the constraints of a recorded history, the past cannot be literally constructed; it can only be selectively exploited. Moreover, the basis of the exploitation cannot be arbitrary. The events selected for commemoration must have some factual significance to begin with in order to qualify for this purpose."[22] These observations, however, are not without controversy.

Indeed, a retreat to the past, while problematic in its own right, seems a rational alternative when faced with the challenges of an alien and unfinished present. We have all at one time or another longed for a more simple time when the day to day challenges of our lives could be held at bay by the serenity of the our youth and the effortlessness of a warm summer evening. Of course, those things too occur less in fact and more so in the fictional accounts we use as a default mechanism to ward off the stark reality of daily life and often consign us to long for something that by its very definition never existed in the first place. Nevertheless, and this is perhaps even more of a conundrum for those of a more sport-minded air given sport's propensity for cross-generational assessments and the personalizing effects of embracing a team or a game or even a moment, harkening back can be a comfortable and comforting refuge, but it too comes complete with a set of ambiguities that suggest that the haven was anything but safe and that the shelter was indeed full of holes.

The situation as described above regarding Robinson and his legacy within the confines of contemporary nostalgia and its resulting confusion as well as the formative value that can be gleaned from it all leave this chapter of the self-narrative exposed to corrupting elements that are contraindicated and as equally woefully beside the point. By removing the contextual elements of Robinson's circumstances, and by instilling in their place an artificially constructed narrative placed squarely within the confines of more modern settings, we deprive ourselves of the very thing we wish to embrace and then wonder why it is that we can never measure up to such challenges, especially as an increasingly bleak future continues to unfold before us. As Columbia's Jeffrey Orlick explains, "Now, since the end of the twentieth century, we experience a memory boom in which novelty is associated with new versions of the past rather than with the future."[23] Or to borrow from the sports world, the situation as we foresee it has become a veritable mismatch.

A CHALLENGING ICON

The contradictory and often misaligned nature of Robinson's legacy is well chronicled in many of the more recent works and certainly subject to the permutations as expressed here thus far. For example, in the introduction to a 1997 collection of essays, editor and eminent Robinson scholar Jules Tygiel notes that while Robinson's rise from curiosity to national phenomenon in 1947 was rather swift, such a leap was not without its disquieting subplots. He explains: "Although few people realized it at the time, Robinson had also launched a revolution in American athletics . . . [but by the late 1960s] [s]ports became the primary symbol of social mobility in the black community, prompting concern about an overemphasis on athletics among African American youth."[24] This dual treatment of Robinson is actually a common occurrence in much of the literature. To be sure, Robinson's life offers a mass of contradictory assertions, many of which would prove, oddly enough, vital to his material success both on and off the field in spite of the more obvious incongruities. Indeed, much of the more critical analyses show Robinson to be a man quite conflicted with regards to many facets of his own life, a brief accounting of which I'll sum up in the following:

He was, for example, a college-educated man in a milieu that by and large rejected book-learning and learned men. He was an accomplished athlete whose baseball prowess had yet to be fully realized by 1946.[25] He was also a commissioned officer in an armed forces that typically disregarded the African American contribution to

the war effort. Additionally, he was an outspoken man chosen for a role that ultimately denied him the option to defend himself in the face of immeasurable pressure. Beyond that, he was a man prone to liberal causes who embraced capitalism and was strongly allied to the Republican Party when this was becoming extremely unfashionable and faced significant criticism as a result.

He could be on the one hand philosophically Washingtonian in his commitment to self-reliance while concurrently donating his money and his name to political causes in the tradition of a Du Bois or a Dr. King. And he could be highly critical of many black radicals, though he grew to respect their place within the much larger canon of race-based discussions later in his life. In this regard, his running battles with Malcolm X in the pages of *The Amsterdam News*, or his now infamous appearance at the Robeson HUAC hearings certainly attest to the fact that the Jackie Robinson so in vogue today is in many ways not all that reminiscent of the man himself in his own day.

That Robinson could be celebrated nationwide while never seeming to fit any sort of pre-prescribed mold underscores a significant point of friction between those who insist on lionizing Robinson and those who choose if not to dismiss him entirely to certainly discount his place amidst the much larger discussion surrounding race, sport, and linkages within America. While on the one hand Robinson could be positioned as a symbol of change, the ramifications of these changes away from the realm of popular culture alone were not nearly enough to sustain the momentum generated by his initial renown. As Olsen would remark some twenty years after Robinson's surge into the nation's consciousness: "Every morning the world of sports wakes up and congratulates itself on its contributions to race relations. The litany has been repeated so often that it is believed almost universally. It goes: 'look what sports has done for the Negro.'"[26]

The leap from black man in a Dodger uniform to the more substantive-laden civil rights ambitions in terms of, say, housing, education, equal access, etc., is certainly problematic. To be sure, overstating Robinson's role in the promotion of civil rights misses the mark, but undervaluing his contribution to at the very least a creeping awareness of cultural change can be equally sticky. While the former certainly exaggerates the effect that Robinson would have had on progressive elements in American life in light of those who served on the frontline of the struggle, the latter seems to offer its own backward reading of history that threatens not to necessarily force a reevaluation of the role of the collaborative but, rather, serves to eliminate whatever gains have been fostered through the desegregation of America's playing fields *ad hoc*. The suggestion made by some that the upshot of the Robinson story has been to align black progress with athletics is both apt and certainly defensible given the changes wrought over the past forty or so years, but blaming Robinson for these changes is, to paraphrase Harry Edwards arguing in an oddly similar context, the equivalent of picking up the ball but running the wrong way with it.[27]

STAGING BANALITY

The tension between Robinson the pioneering hero and the more critical assessments relative to outcome is indeed significant. In many ways, one can suppose that the dividing line can be construed as racial in nature, though this remains to be fleshed out in its entirety. Still, whereas African Americans may be divided over Robinson and the resultant sport consciousness of generations since, there is a certain and notable degree of self-congratulatory hand-wringing taking shape within the more mainstream spaces of American life. And nowhere was this more pronounced (and perhaps absurd) than in the Boston Red Sox organization's decision to schedule multiple annual celebrations of Jackie Robinson's legacy beginning in 2003.

When I first caught wind of these festivities and learned later that they were happening beyond what had already taken place throughout Major League Baseball, I had to double take. The franchise that had the first shot at him and was the last team to integrate now seems to hold Robinson to its collective breast?[28] Still, and beyond this rather absurd twist, there is the matter of the wide-ranging embrace of Robinson that has swept across a new generation. The impetus to *be like Jack*[29] among the populace has the alternate effect of allowing for a reconceptualization of *racist* as part of a third-person narrative that helps to establish yet another innovative model for the spread of larded national myths that seems remarkably free from the material realities of America's legacy of Jim Crow as it pertained to all segments of American life. Not unlike recent attempts on the part of the German state to distance itself from complicity in the various WWII-related tragedies,[30] today's moralizing elements look to such embraces in order to help rehabilitate its own questionable legacy of bigotry by virtue of celebrations that honor those who in their own lifetimes were often reviled or at the very least subject to the peaks and valleys of wholesale marginalization or thinly veiled insult. To be clear, I am not suggesting that we should not celebrate or refuse to acknowledge the work of past figures but, rather, that when the legacies of the once notorious become caught up in the star-making machinery of popular culture, it gives one pause to reflect upon the meaning of such dramatic transformations. Whether this is a matter of cultural or historical awareness or if it should come under the heading of the more recent trend toward exploring cultural competencies,[31] anytime such a dramatic shift begins to consume an age, it should trigger a more critical assessment that seeks a more material understanding of such a move. And in the case of a modern world so shrunken by vast advances in communication that as far back as 1975 journalist Russell Baker could note that the past we examine is often "so recent that only an eleven-year-old could possibly view it as past,"[32] Connerton in turn can foresee: "We experience our present world in a context which is causally connected with past events and objects, and hence with reference to events and objects which we are not experiencing when we are experiencing the present. Hence the difficulty of extracting our past from our present: not simply because present factors tend to influence—some might want to say distort—our recollections of the past, but also because past factors tend to influence, or distort, our experience of the present."[33]

THE SPORT–RACE CONUNDRUM

Beyond the uniformity of popularly conceived depictions lie the more substantive matters pertaining to sport and blackness and the consequences of Robinson's historic rise. Attempts to clarify sport's more material role in African American life continue to swirl about Robinson's legacy, a matter for which Robinson himself seemed to be conflicted. As he would tell *Look Magazine* in 1957: "Maybe my sons will want to play ball, as I have, when they grow up. I'd love it if they do. But I'll see to it that they get a college education first and meet the kind of people who can help them later. That way, they won't have to worry about getting a good job when they quit playing."[34]

The question of whether or not equal opportunity in sport has been good for black America is indeed complex. Statistically speaking, it is an open secret that the most popular American spectator sports[35] have taken a remarkable turn since Robinson, though these numbers tend to overly reflect labor increases rather than managerial ones. To be sure, escalating numbers of African Americans who play American football, basketball, and to some extent baseball, though the numbers have dwindled significantly of late, often masks the fact that players are not owners, and that the sheer numbers of players alone does not come close to translating into a sort of latent power base diffusing its way throughout American sport. Furthermore, that Robinson didn't live to see Frank Robinson's debut as manager of the Indians in 1975 or the dawning of the age of free agency, though Robinson was conflicted about this earlier on in his post-playing days, is indeed a shame given his open lobbying for such opportunities later in his life. Nevertheless, it would take only a decade or so before the celebration of baseball integration would be muted by the concern that sport had grown to become too much a part of the black community.

While sport may have once appeared as the first likely step on the road to fully realized citizenry, the back-peddling from the age of a strained white athletic superiority (John L. Sullivan, Cap Anson) to the conception of black prowess at an atavistic level (Jack Johnson, Jesse Owens) would lead to an even more problematic set of concerns among race critics. The sport–race conundrum may have been settled on the popular level, but in the trenches where this conflict continues to resonate loudly, this matter is far from resolved, something that the first generation of post-Robinson scholars could note early on in their critiques.[36] As Othello Harris has observed: "While many whites and some African Americans still touted sports' role as an escalator to social mobility for ['ghetto blacks'], many African Americans—athletes and others—began to condemn the sport establishment for blatant exploitation and racial discrimination. No longer would a belief in sport as the route to increased status go unchallenged. If whites had renewed their faith in sports' ability to elevate the status of the black community, they were not joined in this belief by many of those principally involved—black athletes."[37]

In present circumstances, the drive for athletic distinction at the expense of other pursuits has grown to be one of the more hotly contested areas in the pairing of race and sport, and the evidence that supports critical race–sport paradigms demonstrates both quantitatively as well as anecdotally that sport replicates many (if not all) of the same power imbalances found within the greater social structures at large.[38] In other words, whereas limited participation in sport once mirrored larger limitations within American culture in the pre-Robinson era,[39] the post-Robinson era with its massive influx of black athletic celebrity offers a more innovative yet similarly insidious angle in terms of a racialized American order. By tantalizing young men and women with promises of wealth and fame (without benefit of the fine print), sport seems to have become the quintessential Sisyphusian pipedream, but pinning these developments on Robinson or Rickey or even on the nature of sport itself serves to stand logic on its head. Integration through sport may have proven to be a mythological project, but placing the blame on a particular circumstance—in this case Robinson's rise to the major leagues—reveals a similar revisionist design remarkably similar to that demonstrated by those who look to Robinson as the standard bearer of twentieth-century change.

It is interesting that while we can point to a man with a paradoxical nature and perhaps even feet of clay, we can also note that his accomplishments were nothing short of extraordinary as recognized in American cultural idiomatic expression. Tiger Woods in golf and the Williams sisters in tennis were all mentioned at one time or another as Robinsonian pioneers, though often times the convergence of that moniker becomes a stick with which to beat outspoken black athletes back into line. Certainly Woody Strode and Kenny Washington and Fritz Pollard before them, Chuck Cooper, Nat Clifton, Willie O'Ree, Arthur Ashe, Althea Gibson, and to some extent Lynette Woodard would too suffer the slings and arrows of having served in the not necessarily catbird seat[40] of a 1947 Jackie Robinson in their respective times. It is to be sure an enduring image but it does comes complete with its own set of contradictory baggage, baggage that still begs to be sorted out some six decades after the fact.

NOTES

1. Buddy Johnson, "Did You See Jackie Robinson Hit That Ball?" *Baseball's Greatest Hits*. Los Angeles: Rhino Records, 1980.

2. Alan Fotheringham, "Lionizing Athletes Is a Disservice to Blacks." *Maclean's*. 110, no. 15 (14 April 1997): 64.

3. I explore this in much greater detail in my book *The Erosion of the American Sporting Ethos: Changing Attitudes toward Competion* (Jefferson, NC: McFarland and Co., Inc., 2007).

4. David Lowenthal, *The Past Is a Foreign Country* (Cambridge, UK: Cambridge University Press, 1988), 361.

5. Gary Alan Fine, *Difficult Reputations: Collective Memories of the Evil, Inept, and Controversial* (Chicago: University of Chicago Press, 2001).

6. Fine, *Difficult Reputations*, 4.

7. Fine, *Difficult Reputations*, 6. See also Cooley, Charles Horton Cooley, *Social Organization: A Study of the Larger Mind.* (New York: Shocken,1964), 342.

8. Fine, *Difficult Reputations*, 6.

9. Frank Füredi, *Where Have All the Intellectuals Gone? Confronting 21st Century Philistinism* (London: Continuum, 2004). See also James Heartfield, *The 'Death of the Subject' Explained* (Sheffield, UK: Sheffield Hallam University Press, 2002), and James L. Nolan, Jr., *The Therapeutic State: Justifying Government at Century's End* (New York: New York University Press, 1998).

10. Nolan, *Therapeutic State*, 15.

11. This phrase became embedded within the nation's sport consciousness in Jules Tygiel's seminal book that chronicles Robinson's story. See Jules Tygiel, *Baseball's Great Experiment: Jackie Robinson and His Legacy* (New York: Vintage, 1984).

12. See, for example, John Hoberman, *Darwin's Athletes: How Sport Has Damaged Black America and Preserved the Myth of Race* (Boston: Mariner/Houghton-Mifflin Company, 1997). Hoberman's controversial work is among the more recent accounts of the sport myth paradigm, though by no account is the sole proprietor in this particular field. See also Varda Burstyn, *The Rites of Men: Manhood, Politics, and the Culture of Sport* (Toronto: University of Toronto Press, 1999), and Douglas Hartmann, *Race, Culture, and the Revolt of the Black Athlete* (Chicago: University of Chicago Press, 2003).

13. This particular reference as well of the Gertz quote, though paraphrased as well, can be found in Andrew W. Miracle, Jr. and C. Roger Rees, *Lessons of the Locker Room: The Myth of School Sports* (Amherst, NY: Prometheus Books, 1994), 9.

14. As an aside, it is interesting to note that as late as the seventeenth century, cultural critics continued to refer to nostalgia as a disease, one that was more and more indicative of a particularly European context though not necessarily strictly so. See, for example, Svetlana Boym, *The Future of Nostalgia* (New York: Basic Books, 2001), xi and 3–7.

15. Boym, *Future*, 43.

16. Lowenthal, *Past*, 325.

17. Lowenthal, *Past*, 341.

18. Boym, *Future*, 342.

19. Karl Marx and Frederich Engels, *Selected Correspondence*, (Moscow: Progress Publishers, 1975), 93. This quote also appears in Frank Füredi, *Mythical Past, Elusive Future: History and Society in an Anxious Age* (London: Pluto Press, 1992), 72.

20. Füredi, *Mythical Past*, 26, 70.

21. Maurice Halbwachs, *On Collective Memory* (Chicago: University of Chicago Press, 1992), 43.

22. Barry Schwartz, "The Social Context of Commemoration: A Study in Collective Memory," *Social Forces* 61, no. 2 (1982): 396.

23. Jeffrey K. Orlick. Introduction, in *States of Memory: Continuities, Conflicts, and Transformations in National Retrospection*, ed. Jeffrey K. Orlick, (Durham, NC: Duke University Press, 2003), 3.

24. Jules Tygiel, *The Jackie Robinson Reader: Perspectives on an American Hero* (New York: Dutton, 1997), 1–14.

25. Buck Leonard, for one, was shocked by Rickey's choice while others were flat out furious. See Art Rust, Jr. *"Get That Nigger off the Field!" A Sparkling, Informal History of the Black Man in Baseball* (New York: Delacorte Press, 1976), 30–31.

26. Jack Olsen, *The Black Athlete: A Shameful Story. The Myth of Integration in American Sport* (New York: Time-Life Books, 1968), 7.

27. David Leonard, "The Decline of the Black Athlete: An Interview with Harry Edwards." *Color-Lines* 3, no. 1 (2000): 21.

28. Tygiel offers a full recounting of this audition in his aforementioned Robinson work. Tygiel, *Reader*, 39–52.

29. A revised point of reference based on one of Michael Jordan's ubiquitous ad campaigns.

30. See Sabine Reul, "German History on Trial Again" *Living Marxism*, no. 48, October 1992, 29, http://www.informinc.co.uk/LM/LM48/LM48_Oss.html (2 June 2006). Reul, a German national, posits that the increased pressure from within Germany to embrace complicity in the events of World War II masks a cynicism on the part of the German state to relieve itself of any responsibility while allowing other nations who shared similar such race-based ideologies, including the United States, to resolve their individual roles in the carnage as well. See also Füredi, *Where Have*, 41–48.

31. For an interesting perspective on the relatively recent and certainly controversial construct see Ryan Bigge "The Death of the Double Entendre: Ads Are Killing Our 'Cultural Competencies,'" *Toronto Star Online*, 16 July 2006, http://www.thestar.com (19 July 2006).

32. Russell Baker, "Shock of Things Past," *International Herald Tribune*, 2 May 1975, 14. This quote also appears in Lowenthal, *Past*, 6.

33. Paul Connerton, *How Societies Remember* (Cambridge, UK: Cambridge University Press, 1989), 2.

34. Tygiel, *Reader*, 218.

35. Defined here as the ones that offer big payouts to its performers.

36. See, for example, Othello Harris, "The Role of Sport in the Black Community," in *African Americans in Sport: Contemporary Themes*, ed. Gary A. Sailes, (New Brunswick, NJ: Transaction Publishers, 1998), 3–13.

37. Harris, "Role of Sport," 10.

38. Richard Majors, "Cool Pose: Black Masculinity and Sports," in *African Americans in Sport: Contemporary Themes*, ed. Gary A. Sailes, (New Brunswick, NJ: Transaction Publishers, 1998), 15–22.

39. David K. Wiggins, *Glory Bound: Black Athletes in a White America* (Syracuse University Press, 1997), 221–42.

40. To paraphrase Red Barber's famous colloquialism.

ROBERTO CLEMENTE

From Ignominy to Icon
DAVID C. OGDEN

INTRODUCTION

Roberto Clemente was both an enigma and a contradiction. Accused of being a hypochondriac, he played through considerable pain. Labeled a showboat, Clemente displayed defensive excellence and eccentricities, including his Mays-like basket catches, a style of play that evolved from his practice habits as a child. Dubbed a malcontent, Clemente became the on- and off-field leader of a team destined to be world champions. Made out to be a malingerer, Clemente was said by some writers and fellow players to be one of the hardest working players on the team.

Clemente's cultural and social struggles are no less transparent than those of Jackie Robinson, Lary Doby, or other Negro League stars who migrated to the major leagues. But unlike those players, the enormity of the cultural divide that confronted Clemente often left him wholly misunderstood, especially by the print and electronic media that followed him while deliberately framing him as someone outside the community and system. In essence, Clemente was discriminated against not just for the color of his skin but also for his lack of knowledge of the language, the culture, and American society itself. Yet, and in spite of the odds stacked against him, he would nonetheless become one of the most revered figures in the history of baseball in general and in Pittsburgh sports scene in particular.

The media played a significant role in constructing Clemente's mainstream image and how the general American public perceived him. But Clemente had many "subcultural reputations," as sociologist Gary Alan Fine would term them, as well.[1] That is, his reputation varied from culture to culture and from country to country. In his native Puerto Rico, his growing prowess on the field was a point of national pride. In the United States, however, he was an enigma: talented but erratic and sometimes not dependable. But toward the end of his playing days and in the years following his tragic, albeit storied, death, social forces and the insatiable hunger for heroes and legends have resculpted Clemente's reputation while recasting Clemente within the framework of new social and cultural perspectives. The focus of this chapter, thus, is to examine the process by which Clemente's reputation evolved and to offer some explanations for the spike in public interest in Clemente. Examining the images of Clemente early in his career provides a contrast to his legacy today, and exploring the concepts of "reputation" serve as a way to illustrate how the images of historic figures, and in this case historic sports figures, take on new dimensions as time passes and society changes.

THE COMPLEXITY OF CONSTRUCTING REPUTATIONS

In his book, *Difficult Reputations*, Gary Fine describes three approaches for studying what he deems the creation of an historical figure's reputation. Those frameworks are the objective, the functional, and the constructed.[2] The objective approach is based, as Fine explains, on "a world of facts." He notes further that "[i]ndividuals and groups have reputations achieved by virtue of their actions. We judge them by the fruits of their labor and assume that these fruits can be easily evaluated."[3]

The functional model reflects what Fine denotes as *status hierarchies* and the maintenance of social order. In this model, Fine anticipates that reputations evolve as a means to further "help establish the boundaries of society."[4]

In the third approach, the model for socially constructed reputations, Fine posits that reputations are established around *central narrative figures* that result from various social, cultural, and political aim of groups with vested interests. Applying those approaches to an inquest of Clemente's reputation yields a contradictory and sometimes confusing mix. While an objective approach to what Fine calls "the world of facts"[5]—his playing statistics—provides ample evidence of his offensive and defensive prowess (and to his durability at times), the functional and socially constructed models portray a troubled and fragile Clemente, a man who would remain on the social fringes regardless of his profile. Media played a major role in making Clemente a central narrative figure, but their role in the functional approach to Clemente's reputation looms just as large. The press provided the earliest frame for Clemente's image, but events, such as the 1971 World Series, his tragic and premature death on New Year's Eve 1972 and the circumstances surrounding it, and an assortment of social changes would overlay other images of Clemente on the earlier depictions of his contrary nature. To be sure, Clemente's image was crafted to a large degree by journalistic accounts, and he battled that media-constructed reputation as much as he battled his well-reported physical maladies.

Electronic and print media both can hold inestimable sway in forming the public agenda and in contributing to the social construction of reputation, especially when there are no other sources of information.[6] Studies abound in press and media's influence on public perception of issues and individuals. Research has focused on topics ranging from television's role in viewers' construction of imaginary relation-ships with celebrities[7] to the influence of economic news.[8] Fine acknowledges the importance of mass communication in reputation formation when he says that "in any media-saturated society a large and powerful domain of public discourse oper-ates. The media help to determine whom we should know about and care about."[9] Fine, in so many words, describes the social construction theory of agenda setting, in which a primary role for press and media is to tell the public who and what is worth caring about. Moreover, Fine also refers indirectly to media's gate-keeping function in screening news about individuals while setting the agenda by deciding which individuals are notable (and for what reasons) and which should become "topics of conversations among audiences who have never met them, but consider them 'known.'"[10] In terms of the Clemente narrative as it was being constructed, the media made Clemente a topic of conversation by being early instigators in functionalizing Clemente's reputation and marginalizing and categorizing him as a black man. In this regard, Jim Crow was alive and well in 1955 when Clemente joined the Pirates, and he felt the brunt of attitudes toward blacks, attitudes that were embedded in U.S. society.

AN ALL-TOO-EASY TARGET

Although Jackie Robinson's entry into the major leagues in 1947 was a profound moment in American desegregation efforts, it did little to ameliorate racism in many aspects of life. Clemente's arrival in Pittsburgh did not draw the attention that Robinson's did in Brooklyn, but his reputation was also that of the *Other*, as someone foreign to and ignorant of socially accepted customs and behavior. As a result, he faced racism similar to Robinson and in some ways worse. Clemente was not the major league's first Hispanic, but he was a black man among a team and community dominated by whites. Unlike Robinson, he didn't know the language or the customs of American society. Biographer Bruce Markeson describes it as a situation in which "Clemente had said repeatedly throughout his adult career [that] he was a double minority, a fact that left him even more susceptible to rac-ism than his African-American contemporaries."[11] More candidly, earlier Clemente biographer Phil Musick noted that throughout much of his adult life in the U.S., Clemente referred to himself as a "double-Nigger."[12]

In the documentary, "Clemente—21," former Pirate pitcher Nellie King agreed that Clemente's early cultural struggles in the major leagues were probably more difficult than any black man had experienced prior, explaining: "[Jackie] Robinson had to deal with some very serious problems, but Roberto Clemente, as a Latin American, had as many or more problems than Robinson did. Robinson had to face one problem—He was a Black American. He understood the prejudice in this coun-try. Clemente came [and] he didn't understand."[13] Major League Baseball's career home run champion Henry Aaron echoed King's sentiments, noting that "[i]t was probably harder on him [Clemente] than it was on me."[14]

Like other blacks athletes, Clemente received deferential treatment on and off the field. He could not stay with the white players during spring training in the 1950s and 1960s, and whites-only restaurants restricted dining options on the road. Language and cultural differences made him shy away from teammates, many of whom considered Clemente aloof if not altogether antisocial. On some issues, however, Clemente was outspoken. For example, he railed on against the treatment of Latin players, insinuating at one point that racism was a major reason star Latin players were never invited to speak at off-season baseball-related banquets and events. He bristled at teammates and others who called him *Bob* or *Bobbie*, as was fashionable in and around Pittsburgh. According to biographer Bruce Markusen, "Clemente did not encourage such Americanization of his given name, a disrespectful practice that had occurred mostly during the late fifties and early sixties."[15]

Clemente's defense of his Latin peers and his culture early in his career only served to alienate him further from a team and public who already considered him a social and cultural misfit and someone who occupied a low rung in the status hierarchy. Clemente was deviant but not in a moral sense. Rather, he was perceived to be a deviant in a cultural sense, and by not abiding by society's assumptions of appropriate behavior for an athlete (i.e. not complaining, carousing with teammates, displaying a high threshold of pain), his every move was heavily, if not overtly, scrutinized. As a black man, the foundation for his functional reputation marks a reputation that can be driven by what Fine contends are "biological and demographic differences"[16] that can be used by a community in predicting character and behavior. In Clemente's case, those differences were also used to distance Clemente culturally from the community, at least early in his career.

Clemente's reputation as a function of the community's guardedness against those with such differences would not have been as easily formed if not for the uniqueness for which the media portrayed him. To be sure, Clemente's sense of sociocultural dislocation was played out in these spaces. Regarding sociocultural dislocation, De Hoyas et al contend that "minority group members find themselves in a position wherein their values and social structures (particularly their family structure) are far removed from and at variance with middle-class values and social structures."[17] Social work literature has too noted the various self-images individuals carry in defining their sense of place in society and culture.[18] Electronic and print media serve here as a stage displaying the conflict of Clemente's self images, i.e. his personal self-image (the image which one perceives his/her family and culture hold) and his social self-image (the image which one perceives his/her immediate society and its institutions hold of himself/herself). Clemente's personal self-image, which was one of pride in his cultural background and heritage, clashed with his social self-image in which he perceived that news media, business establishments, and society in general had little respect or concern for him and his native culture.

Much more recent Clemente biographer David Maraniss (2006), in quoting former Pirates General Manager Joe L. Brown, said Clemente possessed a " 'huge sense of self-worth, of social self-worth. That he was as good as anyone who ever lived. That people should recognize that he was a special person. He didn't lord it over anybody, he just believed it.' "[19]

Press and media accounts exacerbated this conflict between Clemente's self-image and what he perceived as society's image of him by pointing out his substandard skin color, culture, and language. From his earliest days in Pittsburgh, reporters quoted Clemente phonetically, realizing or not the marginalization to which they were subjecting him. Biographer Bruce Markusen relates how in 1955 Les Biderman of the *Pittsburgh Press* gave the twenty-year-old Puerto Rican rookie's reason, verbatim, of why he wasn't playing to the standards he set for himself: "I no play so gut yet. Me like hot weather, veree hot. I no run fast cold weather. No get warm in cold. No get warm, no play gut. You see."[20] Markusen adds that "such quotations made Latin American players sound unintelligent, almost primitive, and proved distracting to the reader. . . . As a result, the Latino player sounded worse in the newspaper or magazine story than he might have in person."[21] The written media especially pointed to other phonetic foibles and oxymorons by Clemente. For example, in relating to reporters how his chronically aching shoulder felt better than his normally healthy shoulder, the press quoted him as saying "My bad shoulder feels good and my good shoulder feels bad."[22]

Such press coverage served to establish Clemente early in his career as an alien presence and helped to emphasize the cultural and functional differences of people of color. Consequently, the press helped transform Clemente's reputation into one of an antisocial and self-absorbed figure and a representative of a culture that didn't fit. In addition, the press portrayed Clemente as one who didn't care to fit in U.S. society. The press cast such an image when Clemente made an early departure from his World Series–winning teammates' celebration in 1960. Clemente claimed that his swift exit allowed him to be with the people whose admiration he sought—the fans. After the game, Clemente quickly changed, and, according the Markusen, "walked into the mid-afternoon sunshine that enveloped Forbes Fields" to join the throngs of celebrating fans.[23] As former Pirate first baseman and trainer Tony Bartirome verifies: "Clemente liked to be with people. The day they won the World Series in 1960, Clemente left the clubhouse celebration and went outside and went to celebrate with the fans. I'm told that the players held that against him. He wanted to be with the fans. There was some feeling that he should have been with his teammates, that his place was in the clubhouse."[24]

Clemente's defensive style of play, although spectacular, also received criticism from the press for his perceived showboating. As one commentator would note, "In baseball any player who obviously exaggerates simple moves is labeled a hot dog."[25] Clemente most often used a basket catch, positioning the glove below his waist for routine fly balls much like Willie Mays had throughout his own illustrious career.

Moreover, when he wasn't gunning down a base runner, Clemente threw the ball underhanded to the infield, another image that often rankled purists masking what can best be described as racialized agendas. Indeed, some of his over-the-shoulder catches and matching twirls to rifle the ball to third or home have been called by some former players and managers among the greatest outfield defense they have witnessed, matters typically overlooked by the criticizers.[26]

At times, the press recognized Clemente's defensive prowess, such as the *Pittsburgh Press*'s coverage of the 1963 opener at Forbes Field when Clemente charged a Del Crandall fly ball, "dived for it at an angle, caught, did a complete flip-flop and came up with an arm cocked to throw. . . . Eddie Matthews, on third, showed so much respect for the Señor's whip that he made nary a move toward the plate."[27] Yet at times such acrobatics, not to mention his sliding catches and unorthodox base running and batting styles, were translated by the press as examples of a pretentious style. Such a reading by reporters serves again to illustrate how cultural expressions were misinterpreted. Clemente's playing style might be described as a form of what writer Richard Majors meant when he coined the term *cool pose*, in which movement and physical action in themselves serve as a means of communication and self-identity.[28] In discussing the behavioral styles of African American males, Majors claimed that stylistic movements (including walking, dancing, and other physical activity), which may seem grandiose by the standards of some cultures, are means of expression in African American culture, which he termed *cool pose*. Majors claimed that such behaviors that resulted in stylized movements and manners of dress, speech, etc., allow young black males to assert their individuality and distinctiveness and achieve recognition in the face of social and economic obstacles. In Clemente's case, his style of play, like Majors's pose, was perceived as an expression of arrogance or even devil-may-care, and such perceptions illustrate again the conflict between Clemente's personal self-image and the image he knew society had of such seemingly pretentious antics.

Such all-out play often resulted in injuries, but once again press and media's misunderstanding of Clemente and his culture added insult to injury at times. Baseball writer Myron Cope called Clemente a "champion hypochondriac"[29] and explained how Clemente went into great detail about his ailing disc, even flopping on the floor, in response to the question, "How are you feeling?"[30]

An illustration of Clemente that accompanied a Cope article in *Sports Illustrated* included labels placed at numerous parts and areas of his body.[31] The illustration served as an atlas of Clemente's physical complaints. The labels, each strategically positioned in the appropriate anatomical area, included, but were not limited to, nearly every part of his body from head to toe. Included were such maladies as tension headaches, the six stitches he received in his chin after being hit by a ball, curvature of the spine, various stomach disorders, legs that didn't weigh the same, and an assortment of pulled muscles and tendon injuries. But Clemente's professed ailments went beyond the physical. As Cope would remark in 1968, "He is one of the world's greatest insomniacs because he lies awake worrying that he will not be able to fall asleep," lending a further air of incredulity to his litany of injuries while further reinforcing the image of Clemente as the quintessential goldbricker.[32]

What Clemente considered honest and direct responses to reporters' questions was framed as complaining and, when any of his ailments kept him out of the lineup, this could easily be replaced by claims of malingering. As biographers such as Bruce Markusen explain, expectations in Clemente's culture and family were to answer questions in a forthright and open manner. "In citing Clemente's frequent complaints about his physical condition, some writers seemed to be minimizing his sincerity. Although Clemente had once suffered from a serious disease like malaria and had developed bone chips in his elbow—with the validity of each ailment supported by the testimony of doctors—it was as if many writers did not believe that he was sick or hurt."[33] Additionally, Clemente's poor command of English gave writers further impetus to poke fun, sometimes maliciously, at the list of ailments and the way in which Clemente was forced to articulate his hardships both. On one occasion, when Clemente had played well despite his pregame complaints about his physical ailments, he was quoted by one reporter as saying, "I feel better when I am sick."[34]

As a result, Clemente began to shun press and media while trying to make his growing detestation with reporters well known. Late teammate Willie Stargell once noted that Clemente began to castigate reporters for castigating him. Clemente felt that reporters were the only ones who didn't respect his commitment to his team and to baseball. As Stargell would later complain, "The rightfielder had been under a flow of constant criticism for quite some time. The press had accused him of not being a team player."[35] Stargell called such criticism "unfair" while noting: "typical of the media attitude toward Latin ball players, who entered a strange country with strange customs and a strange language and they basically don't know anyone. All they know is how to play baseball. Latin players are proud players and they become hurt when they are constantly made fun of."[36] As Markusen points out, Clemente didn't have the counsel of a media relations expert, and most reporters knew little or nothing about Clemente's culture or background. It was of no surprise then that more than ten years into his major league career, Clemente's relationship with the press corps remained cold, if not icy.

AN ARCHETYPICAL PROVING GROUND

Clemente serves as an excellent example of how the functional approach to reputation can assume new directions. Clemente's skin color, language, and behavior marked him as "deviant" in a blue-collar city and in an American society where the outcry for civil rights was yet to be heard clearly. At the same time, press and media portrayals of Clemente fed into public expectations and perceptions of the deviant *Other*. His brand of deviance faded, however, and his reputation began a slow transformation as he became more accustomed to life in the U.S. and emerged as a team leader by the early 1970s. With his increasing comfort with U.S. lifestyles and language, he became more confident with reporters. As *Pittsburgh Press* reporter Roy McHugh has observed, by the early 1970s, the relationship between Clemente and the press warmed: "Toward the end of his career [Clemente] mellowed and he began to be able to smile at himself." When McHugh inquired about how he was feeling, Clemente no longer detailed his ailments as he might have done in his earlier years. Instead, he offered a light-hearted response. "He would say, 'Oh, I am perfect. . . . If I say I am not perfect, you won't print it anyway.' And then he'd sort of smile and the writers would smile, too."[37]

The softening of Clemente's relationship with the press heralded a shift from Clemente's categorization as a social misfit to a realization that his behavior was the product of a complex and multifaceted personality. In this regard, the 1971 World Series, in which he was voted MVP, served as a catalyst for that shift by drawing national attention to Clemente's objective reputation and his offensive and defensive abilities. In turn, Clemente's death launched a new trajectory for his reputation that continues today.

One of Clemente's roles was not included in the functional or socially constructed frame of early years—his charitable accomplishments. Clemente's humanitarian efforts became the national focus after his fateful mission to earthquake victims in Nicaragua on New Year's Eve 1972 when an aging and overloaded plane took off with relief supplies, Clemente, and four others crashed into dangerous waters shortly after take-off from the San Juan International Airport.[38] His death forced the public to reassess long-held images of Clemente and to consider aspects of the man that before were not considered. Many writers responded to his death like humbled gatherers at a national wake, hat in hands and dignifying a man whom their community had at one time portrayed as clownish and contradictory. The *New York Times* typified the coverage of the 1972 New Year's Eve tragedy when in a January 3, 1973, report they would refer to him as "the most popular figure in [Puerto Rico's] history" and a "certainty to be enshrined in Baseball's Hall of Fame."[39]

In addition to the front-page story, the *Times* devoted a full page to Clemente, in which various sportswriters added to the solemnity: "Since 1955 when he became a rookie outfielder with the Pittsburgh Pirates, Roberto Clemente lived in two worlds and they had one thing in common: passion. On the baseball field he played 18 seasons with passion, often complaining of aches and pains as he attacked National League pitching. Off the field, he would retreat to his handsome house in Puerto Rico to spend the winter with his wife and three sons while resting those aches and pains, but then he would become involved with passion in civic projects until spring training."[40] Sportswriter Leonard Koppett also made references to his devotion and his sense of civic engagement in eulogizing Clemente in that very same edition of the *New York Times*, noting that "Few men, if any, have played baseball better than Clemente did during his 18-year career with the Pittsburgh Pirates. And few players put as much passion into other aspects of life as he did."[41] In retrospect, this remarkable turnabout seems light years away from the man who had been so viciously yet routinely lampooned prior.

Indeed, while Clemente's relationship with press and media had warmed in his last few years, his death was taken as a body blow in the Pittsburgh community. There as well as elsewhere around the nation, Clemente was being viewed in an entirely different frame and one that was certainly contrary to his earlier image. Once cast as introspective and self-centered, Clemente was eulogized by press and media in the days after his death as someone who had made the ultimate sacrifice by attempting to help those less fortunate than him. Such an image is reflected in Koppett's laments that Clemente's death "had more to do with the way he had lived than all of the spectacular baseball statistics for which in due course he will be enshrined in the Hall of Fame."[42]

The refocused posthumous analysis of Clemente by reporters and writers exemplifies the process by which impressions of a person, once formed, can be reformed to reflect changes in public perspectives. That process has been described, albeit at a micro level, by authors Susan T. Fiske, M. Linn, and Steven L. Neuberg.[43] Those researchers have developed the continuum model of impression formation that posits that in forming impressions and, subsequently in this case, reputations of others, people "use a range of impression formation processes . . . , and that the utilized processes depend on two primary factors: the available information and the perceiver's motivation."[44]

To elaborate on this point, Fiske et al. argue that early impressions are usually based on social categories and, especially, "visually prominent categories such as gender, race, and age."[45] Such impressions are formed with little cognitive effort and are done so virtually mechanically by using available heuristics. According to the model, if a person perceives someone of interest, that person often uses those categories and/or other initial perceptions based on preconceived models to in a sense categorize that targeted individual of interest. The categorization remains in effect unless still further information is presented and is contrary to the initial impressions on which the categorization was based. In this case, then, the person may *re-categorize* the individual of interest. In other words, the person may change perceptions of an individual based on new information, but if a person engages in greater cognitive effort in analyzing the individual of interest by sifting through and digesting further information, perceptions will continue to change. Perceptions formed through greater cognitive effort are less likely to change than those perceptions formed in the early stages of categorization and impression formation, when there was little cognitive effort.

Clemente's early reputation, as espoused by press and media, was based on his race and lack of command of standard English usage and idioms. That impression was constantly supported through subsequent media coverage of Clemente's behavioral and linguistic eccentricities. As Fiske et al. points out, "the biasing effects of social categories occur so effortlessly that it becomes difficult to ignore or disregard those effects," though using those categories or personal heuristics, "provides a wealth of information at little cognitive cost."[46]

It is not until new information is introduced or until attention is given to existing, but little known, information that a re-categorization of the person's reputation occurs. Clemente's growing comfort with American culture, the 1971 World Series, and his death the next year all seem to have spurred such a re-categorization of Clemente, and during the ensuing decades, several Clemente biographies have been written and documentaries produced that have presented new analyses of him. Those biographies and video projects have added to a stream of piecemeal information about the Latin star by detailing his fortitude and resilience in the face of prejudice and racism; and as Fiske et al. notes, a greater amount of time is necessary for greater cognitive effort in incorporating piecemeal information into a reassessment of earlier categorizations of an individual.[47]

To be sure, this reassessment continues in earnest. In the past several years, Clemente's image as a Latin pioneer in baseball and as a champion for equal rights has been strengthened through such activities as his 1999 ranking by *The Sporting News* as twentieth among the hundred greatest ball players in history and the White House's recognition in 2002 when he was awarded the Presidential Medal of Freedom. Adding further luster to this shift, in 2003 he was inducted into the U.S. Marine Corps Sports Hall of Fame,[48] and in 2005 he was named a member of Major League Baseball's Latino Legends Team; there are even more indications that this more pronounced reevaluation will gain even more strength.

In 2006 an advocacy group called Hispanics Across America initiated a campaign to retire his uniform number throughout the major leagues, at which some writers balked.[49] Clemente's portrait also graced Wheaties cereal boxes in 2006, a most prominent and cherished honor in American sport culture, and a highly publicized Clemente biography by David Maraniss was also released that year. Such piecemeal information from a variety of sources has molded Clemente's image as that of martyr dying for a cause for which he believed and a hero and legend misunderstood during his career.

Such an outpouring of public interest in the last few years has not been mere happenstance. As this chapter argues and Fiske et al. notes, shifting social conditions do indeed provide a framework for the reassessment of impressions and reputations. According to those authors, social context influences what is perceived and how it is perceived,[50] while several factors have been instrumental in creating a social context conducive to redefining Clemente as a hero. Those factors include:

• The growing number of Latinos in major league baseball (26 percent of players in the MLB are Latino or Hispanic, according to 2004 Racial and Gender Report Card for Major League Baseball.[51]

• The heightened public focus on dying for a cause (via the U.S. involvement in Iraq since 2003 and the constant reminders via news stories in daily and weekly papers across the U.S. about the growing number of U.S. casualties representing all parts of the U.S.).
• A heightened awareness of diversity and multiculturalism in society.
• A continuing need in society for heroes and legends, especially in times of uncertainty and turmoil.

As the continuum model indicates, public expressions of Clemente through books and other media feed into previous assessments of Clemente's image, and in that respect, communication perpetuates long-held reputations or introduces information which may induce changes in reputations. As those expressions continue, in the forms of new Clemente biographies, articles, radio and TV programs, and online contributions, Clemente's image will continue to be renewed, and possibly revamped.

CONCLUSION

Roberto Clemente withstood years of pillorying by press and media, and in the first decade of the twenty-first century, that reputation basks in the glow of re-constructionist research that focuses on Clemente's dignity in the face of scorn. Fiske et al.'s continuum model of impression formation specifies that impressions formed through greater cognitive effort are more resistant to change than those early impressions formed with little cognitive effort. If the model has any predictive value in Clemente's case, his image as an icon and trailblazer for Latin players will remain untarnished for the immediate future, but it remains to be seen what new piecemeal information will be added to the continuing social construction of Clemente via subsequent biographies and research. At the very least Clemente's legacy has fostered a better public understanding of the immense pride Latin players have for their cultures. His legacy has also demonstrated the major role baseball plays in those cultures and the honor Latin players feel in representing those cultures and countries.

There is still much to learn about Clemente. More research is warranted on Clemente as a humanitarian, as someone who had to discover the process of ac-climating to a new land and language, and as a member of the military, serving in the Marines in 1958–59. Such research is either overshadowed or watered down by the focus on Clemente as a ball player. Of even greater interest is Clemente's role as a cultural bridge in educating press and media about how cultural differences affect public perceptions and how those perceptions (and the reputations targeted by those perceptions) change over time. More research on that role might provide new angles for studying the often contrary relationship between today's athletes and press and media. At the same time, such research might further ensconce Clemente as a symbol of Latin integrity and determination.

NOTES

1. Gary Alan Fine, *Difficult Reputations: Collective Memories of the Evil, Inept, and Controversial* (Chicago: University of Chicago Press, 2001), n.p.

2. Fine, *Reputations*, 7–8.

3. Fine, *Reputations*, 7.

4. Fine, *Reputations*, 8.

5. Fine, *Reputations*, 7

6. Joseph T. Klapper, *The Effects of Mass Communication* (New York: Free Press, 1960), n.p.; M. E. McCombs and D. L. Shaw, "The Agenda-Setting Function of the Media," *Public Opinion Quarterly*, 36 (1972): 176–87.

7. N. M. Alperstein, "Imaginary Social Relationships with Celebrities Appearing in Television Commercials," *Journal of Broadcasting and Electronic Media* 35, no. 1 (1991): 43–58.

8. Hanna Adoni and Akiba A. Cohen, "Television Economic News and the Social Construction of Economic Reality," *Journal of Communication*, Autumn (1978): 61–69.

9. Fine, *Reputations*, 9.

10. Fine, *Reputations*, 10.

11. Bruce Markusen, *Roberto Clemente: The Great One* (Champaign: Sports Publishing Inc., 1998), 182.

12. A. Smith and S. Stern, *Clemente—21* [Film] (Black Canyon Productions, New York, 1998).

13. Smith and Stern, *Clemente—21*.

14. Smith and Stern, *Clemente—21*.

15. Markusen, *Roberto Clemente*, 116.

16. Fine, *Reputations*, 8.

17. Genevieve De Hoyas, Arturo De Hoyas, and Christian B. Anderson, "Sociocultural Dislocation: Beyond the Dual Perspective," *Social Work* January–February (1986): 64.

18. De Hoyas, "Sociocultural Dislocation," n.p.

19. David Maraniss, *Clemente: The Passion and Grace of Baseball's Last Hero.* (New York: Simon & Schuster, 2006), 192.

20. Markusen, *Roberto Clemente*, 47.

21. Markusen, *Roberto Clemente*, 47.

22. Markusen, *Roberto Clemente*, 181.

23. Markusen, *Roberto Clemente*, 101.

24. Jim O'Brien, *Remembering Roberto: Clemente Recalled by Teammates, Family, Friends and Fans* (Pittsburgh, PA: James P. O'Brien Publishing, 1994), 92.

25. Myron Cope, *Broken Cigars* (Englewood Cliffs, NJ: Prentice-Hall, Inc., 1968), 255.

26. In their books Markusen and O'Brien provide numerous testimonials about Clemente's circus-like catches and clutch playing.

27. Chester L. Smith, "Tumbling Catch by Bob Clemente Rates as Classic," *Pittsburgh Press*, 14 April 1963: 2C.

28. Richard Majors, "Cool Pose: Black Masculinity and Sports," in *Sports, Men, and the Gender Order*, eds. Michael A. Messner and Donald F. Sabo, (Champaign, IL: Human Kinetics Books, 1990), 109–14.

29. Cope, *Broken Cigars*, 251.

30. Smith and Stern, *Clemente—21*.

31. Myron Cope, "Aches, Pains and Three Batting Titles," *Sports Illustrated*, 7 March 1966, 76–80.

32. Cope, *Broken Cigars*, 249.

33. Markusen, *Roberto Clemente*, 212.

34. Markusen, *Roberto Clemente*, 212.

35. Willie Stargell and Tom Bird, *Willie Stargell: An Autobiography* (New York, NY: Harper & Row, Publishers, 1984), 128.

36. Stargell and Bird, *Willie Stargell*, 128–29.

37. Markusen, *Roberto Clemente*, 227–28.

38. No author, "Clemente, Pirates Star, Dies in Crash of Plane Carrying Aid to Nicaragua," *New York Times*, 2 January 1973, 1, 48.

39. "Clemente, Pirates Star, Dies," 1.

40. Joseph Durso, "A Man of Two Worlds," *New York Times*, 2 January 1973, 48.

41. Leonard Koppett, "Clemente a Player Involved On and Off Diamond," *New York Times*, 2 January 1973, 48.

42. Koppett, "Clemente a Player Involved," 48.

43. Susan T. Fiske, Monica Lin, and Steven L. Neuberg, S.L., "The Continuum Model: Ten Years Later," in *Dual-Process Theories in Social Psychology*, eds. Shelly Chaiken and Yaacov Trope (New York, NY: Guilford Press, 1999), 231–54.

44. Fiske, "The Continuum Model," 232.

45. Fiske, "The Continuum Model," 236.

46. Fiske, "The Continuum Model," 236.

47. Fiske, "The Continuum Model," n.p.

48. J. Correa, "Every Marine Is an Athlete," *United State Marine Corps Sports Hall of Fame Web Site*, 1 August 2003, http://www.quantico.usmc.mil/PAO1/Sentry%20Copy%202003 (21 March 2006).

49. Hal Bodley, "Robinson's Honor Should Stand Alone," *USA Today*, 3 February 2006, 7C.

50. Fiske, "The Continuum Model," 247.

51. Richard Lapchick, *Gender and Racial Report Card for Major League Baseball* (Devos Institute of Business, Florida State University, 2005).

PART II

THE
CHERISHED
DEAD

CURT FLOOD: "DEATH IS A SLAVE'S FREEDOM"[1]

His Fight against Baseball, History, and White Supremacy

DAVID J. LEONARD

INTRODUCTION

With one letter to then commissioner Bowie Kuhn, Curt Flood forever changed his life and eventually the way that Major League Baseball conducted business:

> After twelve years in the major leagues, I do not feel that I am a piece of property to be bought and sold irrespective of my wishes. I believe that any system which produces that result violates my basic rights as a citizen and is inconsistent with the laws of the United States and of the several States.
>
> It is my desire to play baseball in 1970, and I am capable of playing. I have received a contract offer from the Philadelphia club, but I believe I have the right to consider offers from other clubs before making any decisions. I, therefore, request that you make known to all Major League clubs my feelings in this matter, and advise them of my availability for the 1970 season.[2]

In it, Flood had publicly challenged the hegemony of baseball by requesting freedom through the elimination of the reserve clause and a reversal of baseball's antitrust exemption. The reserve clause was brought into being in 1879 by William Hulbert, a coal tycoon turned baseball owner who sought to protect the power of management through minimizing player control and influence on the game. Ostensibly, it allowed for teams to renew a player's contract following each season, which despite violating the basic principles of American capitalism was legal given baseball's antitrust exemption. As Leshanski notes, "In this way all rights to a player's contract belonged to the team and a player could never escape from that club or seek competing bids from other teams. Players were not even able to invalidate a contract by sitting out for a year and then returning to the game. In essence, the club could buy, sell, or trade a player via his contract, as if the player were livestock."[3] While certainly not the first challenge to the reserve clause, Flood's may have been the most effective and determined; his was certainly the most demonized, denounced, and surveilled, which reflects the historic moment of challenge, his blackness, and the realities of American racism.

FLOOD'S ODYSSEY

The story of Curt Charles Flood's fall from grace began shortly after the end of the 1969 season when after twelve productive seasons with the St. Louis Cardinals in which Flood hit better than .300 during six seasons and won seven Gold Gloves, Flood was unceremoniously sent to the Philadelphia Phillies as part of a seven-player deal. Flood described the trade to a losing and undesirable team in a racist city and the subsequent phone call he received from what he determined was a lackey from Major League Baseball's front office as another reminder of his slavelike status. As he would write in his autobiography, "The lightening had struck. The stream lay shattered. It was a bad scene. Feverishly, I harped on my twelve years of service. . . . If I had been a foot-shuffling porter, they might have at least given me a pocket watch."[4] Flood quickly decided that he was unwilling to accept these slavelike conditions, and in order to secure his freedom while maintaining his manhood, he set off on a course that would both symbolically oppose his treatment as a commodity while hopefully changing the actual landscape of baseball. As he put it, he had become "an expert on baseball's spurious paternalism. I was a connoisseur of its grossness. Yet now when the industry was merely doing its thing, I took it personally. I felt unjustly cast out. Days passed before I began to see the problem whole."[5]

As a whole, Flood saw the ways in which management treated and spoke to players; he reflected on the ignorance towards and refusal to deal with racism inside and outside the game. He connected his own experiences, from his trade to management's refusal to give him a raise, to that of the entire league, one where players only took home 20 percent of the league's gross though each represented a piece to a puzzle that invariably showed the realities of exploitation and baseball's plantationlike system. Like a slave, he was "forced to work at reduced wages, [to] sign on the employer's terms, [or be forced] to abandon his career altogether."[6] It was this knowledge and understanding of history, American capitalism, and labor practices that allowed Flood to move beyond persona, to transcend his fight as something more than his avenging the betrayal of the Cardinals. It was a struggle in the long history of African Americans' demanding equality, one that was both carried out in the courts, within the media, and within the court of public opinion.

Although such knowledge and analysis were a driving force behind Flood's struggle, just as were his experiences within the St. Louis Cardinals organization, the historic context of the black freedom struggle and the specifics of black power were equally important to him:

I'm a child of the sixties; I'm a man of the sixties. During that period of time this country was coming apart at the seams. We were in Southeast Asia. . . . Good men were dying for America and for the Constitution. In the southern part of the United States we were marching for civil rights and Dr. King had been assassinated, and we lost the Kennedys. And to think that merely because I was a professional baseball player, I could ignore what was going on outside the walls of Busch Stadium. . . . All of those rights that these great Americans were dying for, I didn't have in my own profession.[7]

Inspired by the courage of Tommie Smith, John Carlos, Harry Edwards, the Black Panther Party, and others engaged in the black freedom struggle, and tired of the exploitation, of "being bought and sold," of being treated as "a piece of property," Flood filed suit against Major League Baseball in 1970.[8] By asserting his sovereignty and demanding his due rights, Curt Flood became an important, oft-misunderstood, actor in the black freedom struggle.

Although an important event in baseball's history and that of the black freedom struggle in America in general, there has been little effort to retell this story. Rather than rehashing this dynamic history, however, the task of this chapter is to reflect on the discursive, media, and historiographic reaction, response, and rememorizing of Curt Flood and his efforts to change baseball. Examining the ways in which the mainstream media chronicled the events involved in his lawsuit, alongside baseball and fan condemnations, this chapter argues that Flood's effort was constructed as neither noble nor heroic, but as rather the destructive acts of an angry, selfish, black militant intent on destroying America's pastime.

The hegemony of this discourse not only reflected the commonsense understanding of race, blackness, celebrity, and sporting cultures but as an emerging white backlash against imagined threats to whiteness. Just as Flood's challenge to baseball's power structure reflected his connection to a larger movement for black freedom, the efforts of baseball and the media to demonize and denounce Flood embodied a societal response to 1960s and 1970s discourses and to those movements for justice. More than giving voice and meaning to these processes of demonization, this chapter works to elucidate the powerful ways in which this discourse impacted Flood himself, repelling the sometimes abstract discussions of white repression. Lastly, this chapter reflects on the powerful ways that Flood's death, more than anything else, transformed the ways in which history, America's sports media, and sporting culture remembered Flood. His death, which resulted in widespread celebration of Flood and his contributions to America, does not, however, reflect progress or even a newfound appreciation of this great man, but rather the continuity of demonization, denigration, and denunciation of blackness in the name of protecting whiteness. The postmortem politics surrounding Curt Flood further exacerbate America's investment in silent black athletes; the contemporary "celebration" of Curt Flood is not a Van Gogh story of honor after death. It is, rather, a sigh of relief for the passing into obscurity of yet another *loud, different, and selfish* black athlete.

DEMONIZATION

From the initial announcement of Flood's intent to sue Major League Baseball, to force change within America's pastime, he was besieged with criticism. At a certain level, the demonization, the cruelty, and the hatred was nothing new, given the daily taunts he faced prior to the lawsuit. From the beginning of his career, Flood faced taunts from fans who used such vulgar insults as "nigger" and "eight ball" during games. Racism within baseball was not limited to fans' screaming racial epithets but evident in experiencing the realities of Jim Crow during road trips into the South with his manager, in privileging white players in terms of playing time, and in the treatment he received from management. As Pat Brady noted on a website dedicated to Flood: "Despite all the ugliness Flood saw at the ballpark and the nation at large, it was no doubt racism in a contract negotiation that shaped his views of the reserve clause."[9]

In 1969, he had requested a raise of ten thousand dollars, after another spectacular season, only to be told that performance notwithstanding the team did not have money to provide for any raises that year. Upon hearing that a white teammate had been given a raise, Flood confronted the general manager: "I was told by the general manager that a white player had received a higher raise than me because white people required more money to live than black people. That is why I was not going to get a raise."[10] Beyond shaping Flood's understanding of the hypocrisies of baseball and demonstrating the deleterious ways in which racism functioned inside and outside of baseball, these experiences elucidated the continuity of racism prior to and subsequent to the lawsuit. The demonization and criticism merely embodied an acceleration of the already blazing fire of American racism.

Not surprisingly many within the media condemned Flood as ungrateful or as yet another uppity and even radical African American athlete who had little concern for either the tradition of baseball or its future greatness. Rather, many in the media painted Flood as both selfish and blinded by both the radicalism of black power and allure of more money. For some, however, his decision was so out-there, so unfathomable in that he was choosing to give up $100,000 per year to play a game, that his sanity was the only possible explanation. Described as crazy, deranged, angry, and even a puppet of union head Marvin Miller, Flood was both demonized and ridiculed by the media and denied agency over and over again.

At the center of the media's reaction were three distinct elements:

• Panic regarding what Flood's attempt would do to baseball, with great emphasis as to how his efforts would result in the demise, if not, destruction of baseball. Unless stopped, he was poised to ruin America's pastime.

• His insertion of race into the discussion. The potential ramifications of his lawsuit were not the sole pollutant in that he used race and deployed the race card long before the race card existed. Rather, it served to potentially disrupt the supposed colorblindness that defined American baseball life.

• Flood's lack of respect and loyalty to the game, which was troubling to them as was his greed and his allegiance to a black identity.

Throughout the media and from baseball itself there was a tremendous focus on how Flood, who at best was crazy and at worse was yet another ungrateful, angry, black militant intent on ruining baseball for white America, would oversee the dramatic altering of this wholly significant American pastime.

Whether manifesting in a backlash against black athletes, black militants, black cultural styles, or hip-hop, culture is historically and ideologically specific, and the panic derived from Flood's lawsuit reflects longstanding and continued practices of fearing black and brown bodies. While writing about recent racialized panics and their intersection with popular culture, Herman Gray persuasively argues that the "discourses of regulation and the moral panics that they helped to mobilize worked for a time in the 1980s to consolidate a neoconservative hegemonic bloc. This bloc routinely used media images of black men and women, the poor, and immigrants to represent social crisis."[11] The demonization and denunciations of Flood, the calls for his being stopped, and the panics that spoke about the end of baseball's tradition certainly embodies this process. In Gray's estimation, hegemonic images, whether those emanating from popular culture or the political pulpit, "became the basis for a barrage of public policies and legislation intended to shore up this hegemonic position and to calm and manage the moral panics construction around race in general and blackness in particular."[12] Others have argued similarly on the intersections of fear, race, moral panics, and calls for state (and perhaps even court and/or baseball itself) intervention. The signifiers of materialism, greed, anger, militancy, and ignorance, all of which are linked to blackness, ubiquitously enter into public discourses as sources of consumption and scorn, as "corrupting and pathological, whether on screen or through welfare debates."[13] Or as Joy James notes, within the American imagination: "[W]hat is forbidden . . . often seems to be projected outward onto the outsider or scapegoat. Blackness has come to represent [an evil within] the national psyche. Although they gain notoriety as the most infamous perpetrators of unrestrained criminality, African Americans are given little recognition in media, crime reports, or social crusades as being victims.[14] The panic as demonstrated here, the imagining of Flood as an outsider destroying an American institution, was not simply a prominent trope within the media's coverage of the Flood case, but reflects longstanding projects directed at blackness.

On January 3, 1970, Flood and Miller appeared on ABC Television as part of an interview with Howard Cosell to discuss his grievances with Major League Baseball in general and the reserve clause more specifically. While somewhat sympathetic to the case, the more typically left-leaning Cosell nonetheless questioned Flood's ubiquitous descriptor of baseball player as indentured servants and slaves, pointing out that $90,000 per year wasn't exactly "slave wages."[15] Cosell gave voice to the widespread populist argument that only questioned the veracity of an athlete claiming exploitation given their immense salaries but played on fan resentment given their own economic position. Without hesitation, Flood reminded Cosell that "a well-paid slave is nonetheless a slave." In other television interviews, Flood continuously reiterated the slavery analogy indiscriminate of fan and media reaction. In one instance, he told a reporter, "What I really want out of this thing is to give every player the chance to be a human being. And to take advantage of the fact that we live in a free and democratic society."[16] In his estimation, the relationship between owner and player was one of "master and slave. As long as you do what I say to do, you're fine; that's great. As long as I can control you and keep your thumb."[17]

Given the efforts of the media and the baseball establishment to bring into focus his $90,000 salary while playing on white resentment toward the black freedom struggle rather than the absence of a free market or the fact that players only secured 20 percent of the industry's total income, Flood faced ample backlash for his referring to baseball players as slaves.[18] In response to Flood's letter to Major League Baseball articulating his grievances, Commissioner Bowie Kuhn wrote in response: "I certainly agree with you that you, as a human being, are not a piece of property to be bought and sold. This is fundamental in our society and I think is obvious. However, I cannot see its applicability to the situation at hand."[19] The fact that Kuhn and others could not comprehend its applicability in this case, just as his denial of the existence of slavelike conditions in the 1970s, is not surprising given the power of whiteness. The erased privileges of whiteness and the perceived increasing power of being black in America facilitated reactions so that Flood's claim of exploitation and slavery were easily dismissed as radical rantings of a truly privileged black male athlete. As such, others were not so diplomatic in their chastising of Flood for his lack of perspective, his anger, his arrogance, and his absurd use of a slave analogy. Indeed, he was mocked as a $90,000 slave.

Dick Young, one of the most influential sportswriters at the time, denounced Flood as selfish and out-of-touch with the struggles of average (read: *white*) Americans. Bob Broeg, a sportswriter for the *St. Louis Post Dispatch*, who covered the Cardinals for years, noted that it would be "difficult indeed to be sympathetic to the little man, particularly when it really is not a matter of principle, but principal."[20] Throughout the press, similar denunciations focused on Flood's use of a slave analogy while wondering, rhetorically, how a man paid so well, a man living the American dream, living out a dream of most American boys, could complain so much and talk so loudly about civil rights. To them and others, Flood's griping was not merely reflective of greedy athletes who took the game and the fans for granted but rather a black power struggle intent on destroying American institutions.

While it may seem as if the reaction or demonizing of Flood embodied a populist sentiment or merely reflected a class divide, media and fan condemnation reflected the centrality of race here. Curt Flood was not alone in comparing the exploitation and experiences of black athletes to those of African Slaves of the eighteenth and nineteenth centuries. Harry Edwards used it often, as did Tommie Smith, Muhammad Ali, and others. More importantly, the use of a slave analogy linked Flood's fight to the public statements of Stokely Carmichael and Malcolm X along with the organizational efforts of the Black Panther Party and other Black Power advocates. The support from the black community, especially the black press, who more often than not linked his fight to a larger struggle against white racism and for black freedom, reflected this common language. Likewise, the white press and many fans had grown tired of such rhetoric, denying the importance of race in this instance. As Pat Brady noted on a website dedicated to Flood: "Flood faced the inevitable position of emerging as a controversial black athlete at a time when much of America had grown tired of controversial blacks. Many in the press condemned Flood as another uppity black seeking merely self-gain and caring little about tradition. Americans felt quite uncomfortable in acknowledging this view that owners tried desperately to spread. Even with all of Flood's talk about principles and morality, much of America alternatingly [sic] saw Flood as a selfish opportunist and the ignorant dupe of the Miller plan to destroy baseball."[21] Or as Belth observes, Flood's playing of the race card and his repeated description of baseball owners as slave owners "brought the complicated and volatile issue of race to the forefront of his case."[22]

Although race always sat at the center of debates and reactions, Flood's repeated use of racially explicit and charged language instigated much outrage from white fans and media types in that it made clear that his fight was not just a response to owner exploitation but one against racism in the game. In this regard, he helped paint America's pastime as not merely an institution marred by labor abuses but as a vestige of white supremacy itself, and as Belth posits, "There were many sportswriters and fans who regarded this kind of analogy as the ultimate sign of disrespect."[23] Thus, Flood's repeated analogy took racism out of the hands of the Klan and other Southern bigots and pointed its fingers squarely at America and more specifically at this supposedly greatest of American cultural shrines. The demonization and condemnation equally reflected a defense of the greatest race-based mythologies surrounding American baseball. Flood, a black man, ultimately challenged the mythologies of whiteness, of baseball being a space of meritocracy and colorblindness, which led America toward racial progress subsequent to Jackie Robinson breaking the color line. As a result, Flood was violating hegemonic beliefs that race had no place in sports while confirming people's frustrations about the increasing ease in which American minorities used race as a strategy or tactic within public debates and policy fights. As University of California Law professor Linda Williams proffers, America's racial history consists of a series of racial crises played out in black and white, one in which panics, cultural battles, and cultural contestations have reflected the ways "in which race cards have been in play in the racial power of games of American culture."[24] Thus, she suggests that to understand Curt Flood's challenge to America's pastime and the reaction to it must take place within the context of a broader racial and cultural narrative. She writes, "It therefore needs to be studied in those places where it made a difference in the American national imaginary: in the ongoing conflicts of racial virtue and villainy that have taken place in the melodramas of black and white."[25]

In erasing power, notions of hegemony, race, and the longstanding racial melodramas that have cast blackness as both a source of villainy as well as a disruptive and destructive force to white cultural spaces, Curt Flood's position showed little difference to others who have followed a similar path. And like so many others, he found too that his challenge to baseball's hegemony, his insertion of race and racism to conversations of exploitation, and his symbolic and actual links to the black freedom struggle were dismissed and recast as unnecessary intrusion of a militant and ungrateful black athlete.

As should be clearly evident, much of the press and countless fans demonized Flood as yet another militant black nationalist athlete who neither respected the game nor the fans while putting themselves and their causes ahead of those who allowed them to play. By this estimation, Flood was clearly ungrateful for the opportunity before him, a sin William Rhoden describes as the ultimate sin for a black athlete.[26] Moreover, he was greedy and ignorant of the game's tradition and was out-of-touch and plainly un-American. As Belth writes, "Part of baseball's powerful myth was that players, especially minority players should be grateful for what the game had done for them and ignore all that those players had done for the game."[27] Flood himself, however, probably best described the level of animosity and anger spewed in his direction, a level of resentment that included daily newspapers' diatribes and death threats in letters addressed "Dear Nigger."[28] As he notes in his autobiography, *The Way It Is*: "Comparatively few newspaper, radio, and television journalists seemed able to understand what I was doing. That a baseball player would pass up $100,000 year was unthinkable. The player's contention that he was trying to serve a human cause was somehow unbelievable. Who had ever heard of anyone giving up $100,000 for a principle? For them the only plausible explanation was derangement. Or perhaps I was a dupe."[29]

A cartoon that appeared in the *St. Louis Dispatch* equally encapsulated both this sentiment and the anger directed at Flood. In it, Marvin Miller sits in the background watching as Flood stands in front of an easel painting a picture. The canvass contains only a dollar sign, to which he appears to be saying "It keeps coming out that way."[30] In other words, no matter the rhetoric offered by Flood, the various smoke and mirrors, he was driven by money and a lack of respect for the game, its tradition, and its fans. Denounced as yet another greedy athlete and another loud and angry black male, Flood was the ultimate pariah in baseball. Alex Belth describes the level of opposition and outrage directed at him as life changing and life defining:

> The pressure on Flood was severe. He was not a media darling like Ali or an intimidating presence like Bill Russell, and he was now facing a level of public scrutiny that was unlike anything he'd ever encountered on the playing field. Flood received various letters, the overwhelming majority of which were supportive. However, it was the small quantity of hate mail that stuck with him, causing him to lose sleep. He was going to destroy the national pastime, they said. One stated, "Once you were compared with Willie Mays. Now you will be compared to Benedict Arnold.[31]

To Belth, Bob Gibson, Jackie Robinson, and Flood himself, the decision to oppose the baseball establishment, to invoke analogies of slavery, to make visible his blackness, the whiteness of baseball, and the ubiquity of racism forever changed Flood's life, resulting in his symbolic lynching by the baseball establishment and departure from America. Within American sporting cultures and within its surrounding media discourses, black bodies are routinely, writes Ronald Jackson in *Scripting the Black Masculine Body*, "treated as 'throwaways'; they are bodies contained in the name of justice. By apprehending power via policing and legitimate authority, and by controlling public perceptions about these bodies, negative discursive representations of them become paramount."[32] Better said, the denunciations and demonizations of Curt Flood, Muhammad Ali, and other rebellious slaves relegated to the sporting plantation, as Flood might have deemed them, the demands for policing of athlete behavior, and the celebration of a since-deceased Flood as a means to condemn black athletes in the twenty-first century jointly serves as vehicle for a modern form of lynching, one that offers prohibitive and sociocultural penalties to those racialized bodies that are not in "alignment with what it means to behave 'normally.'"[33] As Robyn Wiegman argues, "Lynching is about the law . . . the site of normativity and sanctioned desire, of prohibition and taboo. . . . Lynching figures its victims as the culturally abject."[34]

Arguing that the treatment of Curt Flood amid his lawsuit and the rhetorical lynchings that facilitated his exile from baseball and, subsequently, the United States, and the celebration of his fight as the means to control and demean the newer generation of black athletes represents another instance of lynching whereupon black bodies are imagined as abject and dangerous while necessitating a spectrum of control and regulation. Thus it becomes clear that racialized discourses impacted and affected Curt Flood in life while haunting him to his death. And yet, by 1990, Flood's place within American racial and sporting discourses had changed dramatically. No longer a Benedict Arnold or a Malcolm X in a baseball uniform, Flood had been transformed into part Jackie Robinson, part Arthur Ashe, and part Martin Luther King with, of course, Gold Gloves and a wonderful lifetime batting average as the ultimate symbol of American racial progress.

CELEBRATION

Although there was a tremendous backlash against Flood, one that reflected long-standing practices of demonization and vilification of (non)conforming black male athletes, Flood also experienced a certain amount of public support. As already mentioned, both the black press and civil rights leaders celebrated his courage while voicing support for his cause and his efforts.[35] While less vocal, given fears of re-percussions, players, particularly those who retired and those who were African American, publicly supported Flood's lawsuit.[36] Lou Brock has stated that all of his Cardinal teammates were behind Flood, although most were somewhat uncertain as to how to show their support. Indeed, Brock, like Dal Maxvill, Ritchie Allen, Bob Gibson, and dozens of others, quietly allied themselves with Flood, but did so fully aware of the ramifications of being painted with the same brush. Others, such as Jackie Robinson, who had once been on the record as opposing free agency (see Robinson Chapter), were less reticent with their support and celebrated Flood's battle with Major League Baseball. As Robinson would announce: "I think Curt is doing a service to all players in the leagues, especially for the younger players coming up who are not superstars. All he is asking for is the right to negotiate. It doesn't surprise me that he had the courage to do it. He is a very sensitive man concerned about the rights of everybody. We need men of integrity, like Curt Flood and Bill Russell, who are involved in the area of civil rights and who are not willing to sit back and let Mr. Charlie dictate their needs and wants for them."[37] While interesting that Robinson celebrates Russell and Flood, rather than Ali, Smith, and Carlos, positioning Flood outside the company of those more visibly denigrated radical athletes, the support from Robinson was not only important amid the fight but a direct challenge to the media attacks against Flood.

Support was not limited to the black community. Although needing to be convinced that Flood was doing it as a baseball player rather than as a black man, the executive board from the player's association (all but two of its members—Reggie Jackson and Roberto Clemente—were white) backed his fight. He also received support from several prominent white sportswriters, including Jim Murray, Red Smith, Larry Merchant, Milton Gross, Robert Lipsyte, and Leonard Koppett. Larry Merchant penned, "A Matter of Principle" for the *New York Post*, where he not only offered support for the cause and celebrated Flood's courage but argued that Flood's experience with American racism provided him with the necessary perspective to fully comprehend the injustice of the reserve systems, to see its connection to slavery. In other words, his experiences with racism within baseball and through his life, as opposed to those of baseball owners, sports commentators, and fans, whose white privilege clouded their ability to understand Flood's fight and the repeated rhetoric about slavery, demonstrate the centrality of race. Milton Gross, also in the *New York Post*, described the historic significance of the case, explaining to his readers that what Flood was taking on in this battle was "not only suiting for himself, but for the free agent kid, the rookie, the fringe player, the star, and the superstar."[38] Responding to the ubiquitous claims that if successful Flood would not only change the game of baseball, but erode its tradition, Leonard Koppett penned a powerful commentary that offered support for Flood and his case while challenging the basic premise that baseball could remain an immutable pastime rather than serving as a cultural institution that has evolved and changed over time in face of resistance, social transformation, and challenges to its shortcomings:

As for "baseball as we know it"—as who knows it? And when?

Is baseball as "we" know it sixteen teams playing 154-game schedules, twenty teams playing 162-game schedules or twenty-four teams playing in four divisions with play-offs to decide pennant winners?

Is it independent minor-league teams and free competition for new players, or subsidized minors with free-agent draft?

Is it unlimited control of hundreds of players by any one farm system, or an "unrestricted draft" that limits certain control to the forty-man roster?

Is it a half-century of immovable franchise crammed into eleven cities in the northeast quadrant of the country, or sixteen changes in the major-league map in the last seventeen years?

Is it a game played on natural grass or on a synthetic surface? Is it one which starting pitchers complete 75 percent of the game or 25 percent? It is a game where men who hit .400 fail to win a batting title or one in which a man with .301 does? Is it a lively ball or a dead ball, symmetrical stadia or old ball parks, big gloves or little gloves, 400 major-league players or 600 major-league players, with a legal spitball or without, with two umpires on the field or four, under lights or all in the daytime?

The reserve clause has been 100 percent effective since 1915, when the Federal League folded. All the above changes have come about since then. The only aspect "preserved" by the reserve system is the reserve system itself.[39]

In retrospect, Koppett may have also asked whether or not Major League Baseball, as he knew it, is an all-white confederation whereupon African Americans were relegated to the Negro Leagues or those of Mexico and Cuba? Or is it, in the context of both 1969 and the present day, a game or institution that has rules in place, which limits access to those in the United States, or is it one that brings in talent from the entire world, thereby destroying the leagues and talent pools throughout the world? Better yet, is the *game we know*, a game in which players are compelled to use speed or cocaine or maybe even steroids to get an edge, whereupon once again blackness, in the form of Barry Bonds, appears alongside a discussion of pollution regarding selfish players and their myopic attempts to destroy of the tradition of Major League Baseball, an anger the likes of which Curt Flood once elicited, that becomes an ontological sign of decay? So while Koppett is emblematic of the defense and subsequent reclamation of Flood, one has to question the broader significance given the persistence of both tropes concerning the traditions and authenticity of the game, and the persistent indictment of black bodies who threaten the purity of the game.

Notwithstanding, the widespread demonization of Flood as being selfish and out-of-touch, these authors emphasized his courage and selflessness while not only voicing support for Flood's fight and opposition to the reserve system but celebrating the man and his principles. Still, it wasn't until his death, until he was no longer a threat but rather a symbol of America's progress, of baseball's departure from its ugly past, and of the failures of contemporary (black) athletes did Flood receive widespread recognition and praise.

I should like to note here that Flood signed with Washington Senators in 1970 due to the financial difficulties inherent to the cause, but Flood also received immense criticism from the media and fans alike. During a trip to New York, for example, he returned to the clubhouse only to find a black wreath hung in his locker. He would also receive countless letters that referenced the fact that he was a target of not only vitriol but outright physical harm as well. The media denunciations also increased following his signing with Senators, which to many columnists was proof that he was neither principled nor driven by a larger cause but rather motivated by personal greed.

Having failed to convince a federal judge of the merits of his case and tired of the scrutiny and threats of violence he experienced each and every day, however, Flood fled the United States in April 1971. At the airport, he even took a moment to send a short telegram that read simply, "I tried. A year and a half is too much. Very serious personal problems mounting every day. Thank you for confidence and understanding."[40]

While he was living in Spain, the Supreme Court, however, ruled in his case, upholding baseball's antitrust exemption in a 5–3 decision, preserving the reserve clause until 1975, at which time arbitrator Peter Seitz awarded free agency to Andy Messersmith and Dave McNally. The vindication of Flood's efforts did not spawn celebration or even recognition of Flood's struggle as the necessary precursor to that of Messersmith and McNally, at least not until his death in 1997 from throat cancer.

In the days (and years) after his death, and in a most strange turnabout, articles appeared in newspapers, magazines, and on websites throughout the country celebrating both his courage and his contributions to the world of American baseball. Henry Schulman wrote in the *San Francisco Examiner* that Flood "left a legacy of fairness."[41] Notwithstanding the absence of financial rewards or respect while alive, others described him using terms such as pioneer, hero, legend, and freedom fighter—a sort of all-star in the world at large. The man who was daily denounced and virtually banished from America has since been compared to Dred Scott, Jackie Robinson, and Rosa Parks as a great American. George Will encapsulates this celebration not just of Flood, but his contributions to the formation of a just and colorblind America. Celebrating the fact that Curt Flood was able to finally receive his Gold Glove Award from 1969, which he had been unable to receive due to the lawsuit, Will found great pride in the life work of Flood and in a transformed America: "Beneath the strife and turmoil of the baseball business, the game—the craft—abides. It is a beautiful thing, the most elegant team sport. And few have ever matched the grace and craftsmanship Curt Flood brought to it as a player. However, none has matched what he did for the game as a citizen. . . . He once said, 'I am pleased that God made my skin black, but I wish He had made it thicker.' Friends of baseball, and of freedom, are pleased that he didn't."[42]

Amid this new-found praise and reclaiming of Curt Flood as an American hero, many in the sports media began calling for his induction into Cooperstown. *Time Magazine* went so far as to name him one of the 10 Most Influential Sports Figures of the twentieth century, and he would be similarly lionized throughout the nation in other ways. Bill Patterson, for example, founded the Curt Flood Committee, which was dedicated to properly paying tribute to Flood. It oversaw the renaming of a field in his hometown of Oakland, California, as Curt Flood Field, the construction of a statue in his honor, and the establishment of a scholarship in his name as well as his induction into the Bay Area Hall of Fame.

In 1998, Congress passed the Curt Flood Act, which removed Major League Baseball's exemption from antitrust laws as it related to players' rights. Concerned with labor relations by providing players with the same legal rights and statutory protection as other athletes, the Curt Flood Protection was introduced the day after Flood's death by Senator Orrin Hatch, who stated that "the time has come to finish what Curt Flood so courageously begun."[43] Interestingly, only after losing his battle to cancer were baseball, the media, political leaders, and America as a whole ready to accept such a complex individual as Flood. Only after receiving hundreds of death threats; only after years of venomous columns and commentaries within the media; only after struggling with destitute poverty, paralyzing depression, and without acceptance from the game he transformed, and, ultimately, his death, did Flood begin to experience the duality of recognition and celebration.

ANALYSIS

What is revealing in Flood's discursive transformation from ungrateful upstart, destroyer, and troublemaker to hero, legend, and pioneer, is the specifics beyond/ within this process. It is not simply a result of his doing or of his no longer existing as a threat and thus no longer being a dangerous black male; the changed perception is not reflective of a change in American racial consciousness. With rare exceptions, it is important to note how much of the media erased his place within a larger revolt of the black athlete. Focusing on his individual courage and contributions within these post debate celebrations, which tended to imagine him as a superhero, these commentaries virtually ignored the importance of the larger struggle of black athletes and Flood's fight as part of a larger fight for black freedom. Likewise, with rare exception, the discourse tended to minimize, if not discount, the importance of race and identity as it related to both his fight and the subsequent societal reaction. In fact, amid the celebration, numerous authors expressed shock at the media and fan reaction to Flood's American fight, unsure as to how people could demonize and denounce a struggle over fair market capitalism. To them, his fight was class-based, one that linked players, regardless of race, against owners. For example, in an article about so-called game changers, those athletes who left a "profound and revolutionary impact on sports," David Cone celebrates the importance of Flood's fight as "one that brought *us* from almost slavery to modern day free agency."44 Although motivated by racism inside and outside of sports, and inspired by the courage of Edwards, Ali, Carlos, Smith, King, Carmichael, Cleaver, Malcolm X, Newton, Brown, and even Ashe, this post-death discourse saw little significance in race or the history of black resistance. Although he was linked to other so-deemed black troublemakers and agitators, his fight in their estimation was that of a base-ball player. Although he received letters that began "Dear Nigger," and used slave analogies within his fight, the vast majority of articles in an effort to reclaim Flood in a colorblind America celebrated him as a courageous man for whom race means little now when it shouldn't have meant anything then. He was hated then because of racism yet now loved because of and evidenced by the fact that we see him as a baseball player first and as a black man in America second.

Another revealing dimension of the celebration is the erasure of long-term conse-quences and repercussions he faced as a result of his courage because as a black man, his challenge was against the white establishment. There was almost no mention of the death threats and the forced exile; even fewer discussions of the lost income and obsolete chance of enshrinement into the Hall of Fame. Prior to his death, he told *San Francisco Chronicle* columnist Joan Ryan, "If you do what I did to baseball. If you destroyed the underpinnings of this great American sport, you are a hated, ugly, detestable person."45 Interestingly, the few discussions of the devastation and pain that Flood experienced because of the fight were used by a columnist as a point of celebration. They could note, with some irony, how he had lost so much, and yet he could also maintain that he wasn't bitter nor angry at either baseball or America. Indeed, he remained grateful and heroic because he persevered in spite of these obstacles. More importantly, he seemingly holds no grudges.

Lastly, and probably most revealing, the many articles that have appeared since his death in 1997 have said as much about Curt Flood as the ideal athlete as they have about the evils and shortcomings of today's (read: black) athlete. For example, the *Houston Chronicle* published a special section describing Flood as a pioneering figure in the fight for free agency in sports. The authors predictably spoke of his life being a tragedy because of the refusal of those who followed to either match or recognize his courage and contributions.

Of all the millionaires Curt Flood helped make, when Flood succumbed to cancer last January, not a single contemporary player attended his funeral.

Not Shaquille O'Neal, he of the $110 million free-agent contract with the Los Angeles Lakers. Not Chad Brown, of the $24 million free-agent contract with the Seattle Seahawks. Not Albert Belle of the more than $50 million free-agent contract with the Chicago White Sox. Not anyone. Sadly, Flood experienced in death the kind of neglect and solitude he once knew in life.[46]

In their estimation, as with many similar such pieces, the greatest offenders or purveyors of historical amnesia were those who most benefited from his effort. As Jonathan Leshanski would note in a four-part series on Curt Flood that would serve more so to denounce the contemporary athlete: "If you were to ask most of today's baseball players about who Curt Flood was or what he did for them you'd more than likely get a blank stare, although, it is possible that a few of them may be able to tell you that he was a baseball player. The same would probably hold true if you posed the question to most fans. Ironically, what most of these baseball players and enthusiasts do not know is that Curt Flood may have had more influence on modern baseball than any other individual."[47] While today Flood can be viewed as courageous and willing to risk all for a cause, today's athlete can easily be spun as selfish and concerned only with money and material possessions. Flood in death can be humble and can give up everything to make baseball better whereas today's player is loud, arrogant, and shows little concern for the good of the game. As Belth argues, "Flood's sacrifice had gained currency among older journalists who used his stand and subsequent lack of recognition as a platform to criticize modern players as self-centered and materialist—ironic, given how Flood was portrayed at the time of his trial."[48]

To be sure, the story of Curt Flood is certainly one of courage and resistance, but it is equally a story of power, of the powerful and the great lengths the powerful have gone to maintain that control, those privileges and traditions that guaranteed their hegemony. In the end, however, only death could save him from the demonization, from the alcohol and drugs that invariably served as an antiseptic for the pain and poverty, from the letters and stares, from the exile, banishment and denunciations. This part of the story found little place in the reclamation projects that dominated the landscape following his death, but they certainly bear our attention in a time of increasingly reactive and certainly even reactionary narrative.

NOTES

1. Nikki Giovanni, "The Funeral of Martin Luther King Jr.," *The Selected Poems of Nikki Giovanni: 1968–1995* (New York: William Morrow, 1996), 41. With her poem Giovanni elucidates the varied meaning of life and death within a white supremacist America. Voicing sorrow and celebration, Giovanni uses

Dr. King, whose life was defined by his ceaseless effort to taste freedom, to secure freedom for his brothers and sisters throughout the Black Diaspora and in doing so heal the nation, to illustrate the precarious position that has long faced black America. King, like so many African Americans, such as Curt Flood and many of those athletes discussed within this collection, never experienced full citizenship, national love and respect, and most importantly freedom while alive, only able to experience true freedom and power upon death. As such, she concludes that King only reached his promised land, tasting freedom on death's door, demonstrating that "Death Is a Slave's Freedom."

2. Curt Flood, *The Way It Is* (Washington: Trident Press, 1971), 194–97.

3. John Leshanski, *What Every Baseball Fan Should Know: The Curt Flood Case, Part 1*, 28 May 2003, http://www.athomeplate.com/flood.shtml, (14 March 2006).

4. Flood, *The Way*, 187.

5. Flood, *The Way*, 188.

6. Flood, *The Way*, 134.

7. Alex Belth, *Stepping Up: The Story of All-Star Curt Flood and His Fight for Baseball Players' Rights* (New York: Persea Publishers, 2006), 151.

8. Flood, *The Way*, 194.

9. Pat Brady, "As a Ball Player: Flood and Black Power," 21 December 1997, http://xroads.virginia.edu/CLASS/am483_97/projects/brady/black.html (14 March 2006).

10. As quoted in Ken Burns's *Baseball: A Film by Ken Burns* (New York: PBS Home Video).

11. Herman Gray, *Cultural Moves: African Americans and the Politics of Representation* (Berkeley: University of California Press, 2005), 24–25.

12. Gray, *Cultural Moves*, 24–25.

13. Gray, *Cultural Moves*, 135.

14. Joy James, *Resisting State Violence: Radicalism, Gender, and Race in American Culture* (Minneapolis: University of Minnesota Press, 1996), 127.

15. Belth, *Stepping Up*, 158.

16. Belth, *Stepping Up*, 158–59.

17. Belth, *Stepping Up*, 159.

18. Flood, *The Way*, 135.

19. Belth, *Stepping Up*, 157.

20. Belth, *Stepping Up*, 159.

21. Pat Brady, *As a Ball Player*, n.p.

22. Belth, *Stepping Up*, 159.

23. Belth, *Stepping Up*, 159.

24. Linda Williams, *Paying the Race Card: Melodramas of Black and White from Uncle Tom to O. J. Simpson* (Princeton: Princeton University Press, 2001), 4.

25. Williams, *Paying the Race Card*, 297.

26. William C. Rhoden, *Forty Million Dollar Slaves: The Rise, Fall, and Redemption of the Black Athlete* (New York: Crown Publishers, 2006), 226–27.

27. Belth, *Stepping Up*, 159.

28. Flood, *The Way*, 197.

29. Flood, *The Way*, 197–98.

30. Brady, *As a Ball Player*, n.p.

31. Belth, *Stepping Up*, 162.

32. Ronald Jackson, *Scripting the Black Masculine Body: Identity, Discourse, and Racial Politics in Popular Media* (New York: State University of New York Press, 2006), 80.

33. Jackson, *Black Masculine Body*, 56.

34. Robin Wiegman, *American Anatomies: Theorizing Race and Gender* (Durham: Duke University Press, 1995), 81–83.

35. Belth, *Stepping Up*, 198. Although honored by numerous civil rights organization, Flood never felt fully appreciated and respected from the black and civil rights communities, especially in comparison to other athletes who challenged the sporting/American establishments.

36. Belth, *Stepping Up*, 172–73. Bob Gibson described the situation as where players tended to support Flood in private rather than on a public stage, given the feelings of owners, the media, and fans: "The reason nobody backed Curt up is because he was more or less expelled, blackballed from baseball, and it would have happened to anybody else too." Dal Maxvill added: "I still had a few more years that I wanted to play without having the ownership of baseball not happy with me, so I probably wouldn't have enough courage to do that."

37. As quoted in Flood, *The Way*, 196.

38. As quoted in Belth, *Stepping Up*, 160.

39. As quoted in Flood, *The Way*, 205–6.

40. Belth, *Stepping Up*, 180.

41. Henry Schulman, "Fight Ends for Flood," *SFGate.com*, 21 January 1997, http://www.sfgate.com/cgi-bin/examiner/article.cgi?year=1997&month=01&day=21&article=SPORTS12569.dtl (14 March 2006).

42. George Will, *Bunts: Curt Flood, Camden Yards, Pete Rose and Other Reflections on Baseball* (New York: Scribner Publishing, 1998), 279.

43. Pat Brady, "Heading Home: Legacies," 21 December 1997, http://xroads.virginia.edu/class/am483_97/projects/brady/legacies.html (14 March 2006).

44. Mark La Monica, "Game Changers," *Newsday.com*, 30 January 2006, http://www.newsday.com/sports/ny-gamechangers,0,5860259.story?coll=ny-relateditems-sports (17 May 2006).

45. Brady, *Heading Home*, n.p.

46. No author, "Breaking Barriers: Freedom Fighter (Curt Flood)," *Houston Chronicle*, 15 April 1997, http://www.chron.com/content/chronicle/sports/special/barriers/flood.html (17 May 2006).

47. Leshanski, *What Every Baseball Fan Should Know*, n.p.

48. Belth, *Stepping Up*, 200.

PAUL ROBESON

Honor and the Politics of Dignity
PROSPER GODONOO

INTRODUCTION

Scholar, activist, and performer *par excellence*—Paul Robeson was the first twentieth-century African American to be both a popular cultural icon and a hero. A Renaissance man in every sense but long before it would ever be applied to an African American, Robeson became a commodified symbol of blackness that whites felt comfortable consuming while also proving himself to be a fitting and emblematic voice for a community longing for the sort of leader who would not give in to either white authority or oppression.

Throughout the 1930s, Robeson was one of the best known—if not the best-known—Americans abroad. His chiseled features were seen throughout Europe in such American-made films as *The Emperor Jones* (1933) and *Show Boat* (1936) as well as in concerts, stage performances, and European-produced features such as *Song of Freedom* (1936), *King Solomon's Mines* (1937), and his personal favorite, *The Proud Valley* (1940). With his picture splashed over dozens of European newspapers, his enormous presence dominated coverage of concerts, exhibit openings, and receptions for the rich and the famous. Additionally, Robeson would go on to conquer the European stage, becoming the first black man since Ira Aldridge to perform the lead in a 1930 English production of Shakespeare's *Othello* and then returning again in 1933 to critical acclaim in Eugene O'Neill's *The Hairy Ape*.

Robeson's celebrity coupled with his lifelong pursuit of civility, equality, fairness, and humility brought him in contact with people of varying backgrounds and cultures. His vast interests touched many and enabled him to form alliances with the likes of Albert Einstein, W. E. B. Du Bois, Andre Malrux, John Strachey, Kwame Nkrumah, Jomo Kenyatta, to name but a few. More importantly, he—as they—believed that the Western World was failing in its promise to transform the racial climate and conditions for people of color. Still, the more outspoken Robeson became about sociopolitical and cultural issues through his attendant activism, the more his own home country would determine that his brand of activism was inherently dangerous.

Nevertheless, while Robeson's prodigious talents would indeed span the spectrum of the performing arts, one of the images that hovers—perhaps too lightly—about the Robeson legacy was his athletic prowess. The fact is that whatever he might have left us in terms of his activism and his sheer talent spread through his various other pursuits, Robeson enjoyed an unprecedented run as one of early twentieth-century America's greatest athletes, which by every account would serve as the jumping-off point for his illustrious career.

In attempting to bring a measure of clarity to Robeson's place among America's most inspiring athletic icons, let us first recall that Robeson was one of only a handful of African Americans who were able to emerge from the anonymity of Jim Crow sport—if only for a brief moment—and make a name for himself on the broader American sporting scene. Though this aspect of his legacy tends to be shoved aside for many reasons that we shall explore herein, the numbers certainly stand on their own merits. Most conspicuous in this regard is the fact that while at Rutgers University from 1915 to 1919, Robeson was awarded fifteen letters as an intercollegiate participant in football, baseball, basketball, and track and field.[1] Astonishing on its face, this feat would remain virtually unmatched until nearly thirty years later when Jackie Robinson at the University of California at Los Angeles would similarly set the college sports world buzzing when he himself became a four-sport letterman in those very same events. Still, while Robinson's legacy would grow to assume the mantle as one of the most heralded figures of twentieth-century American life, Robeson, his athletic predecessor (and in some ways his political nemesis), remains remarkably entrenched in the shadows.

Attempting to flesh out Robeson's place in the pantheon of American athletic achievement amid the clamor of his seemingly limitless reach in other cultural milieus as well as his infamous run-in with the forces of anti-Communism, thus, can be a daunting task, and primarily because Robeson was so much more than a mere physical presence. Still, there can be no denying his greatness in this particular sphere. As Lou Little, the once-revered football coach at Columbia, whose teams routinely lined up against Robeson, would note, "I think there has never been a greater player in the history of football than the Robeson who was named an All-American end by Walter Camp."[2] In spite of such ringing endorsements, however, Robeson's athletic legacy remains a mere footnote for all but the most ardent scholars and sport aficionados.

That the athletic dimension of Robeson's legacy can be so overshadowed by the many other elements in his life is in and of itself significant and certainly contrary to how modernity constructs blackness through assigning it a physical nature. Moreover, the sorts of omissions that would allow for his athletic career to be all but written out of his life's work foretells that growing sense that while Robeson's legacy may indeed be enjoying a sort of posthumous revival today, the level to which accuracy and illusion blend into plot threatens to render the more notable contributions he once made to a wide range of discussions peripheral if not inconsequential, a matter that hardly does justice to such an inspiring and certainly vibrant figure. Nevertheless, as successive generations continue to grapple with the implications, if not the significance, of Robeson's place in the pantheon of great contributors to American culture, it becomes evident that in spite of the numerous accounts of his life and times, much of what the public thinks it knows about Robeson remains buried beneath the rubble of conjecture and mythology, though his true nature denotes a much more interesting and certainly extraordinary narrative.[3]

RUSHING TOWARD GLORY

If any single scholar-athlete was ever to dispel the racial stereotypes that dominated nineteenth-century thought, it was Paul Robeson. From the athletic fields of his youth to the concert stages of Europe, Robeson's talent seemed inexhaustible and immeasurable and certainly not in keeping with the times in terms of broader discussions of race, class, and measures of success.

Born in Princeton, New Jersey, Paul Robeson was the youngest of four surviving children whose family eventually settled in Somerville, New Jersey, in 1910 where he attended Somerville's colored school. While still in grade school, Robeson first attracted such attention on the local baseball diamonds that he was drafted as a "ringer" to play shortstop for the integrated high school years before he was of age to attend. Thus, it would be at Somerville where Robeson, who was encouraged by his adoring father, William Drew Robeson, a runaway slave whom Robeson affectionately called "Pops," would excel in sports as well as in the classroom where he would be one of only eight students enrolled in college preparatory out of a pool of 250 students.[4]

Just as Robeson's father was to provide inspiration throughout his young life, Robeson's older brother Ben provided the model for athletic performance. The elder Robeson had the ability to make it as an All-American in football or as a professional baseball player, although he ultimately took another path, becoming instead the pastor of the Zion African Methodist Episcopal Church in Harlem, New York, the sort of lust for something more that the younger Paul would certainly display throughout his own life.[5]

With these forces in tow, Paul Robeson continued to ascend athletically, playing forward on the school's basketball team and hurling the javelin and throwing the discus in track and field. But it would be initially on the baseball diamond, where he both caught and played shortstop, that he would make his most lasting impression. It was there too that he would begin to experience what could best be described as full-out racism, accounts of which can be found in the time an opposing manager protested a Robeson triple by shouting "[the] coon did not touch second!"[6] an incident that sparked a major upheaval that was quashed only when Robeson's teammates prevented him from attacking the coach's equally ill-mannered principal.

Incidents such as this aside, and following his numerous high school successes and honors both on and off the field, Robeson entered Rutgers (then College) in the fall of 1915. A private school founded in 1766, Rutgers had only five hundred students, and as only the third black man to attend Rutgers since its inception, Robeson quickly discovered that racism was equally as prevalent in the vaunted collegiate world, a lesson made all too clear when he first tried out for the football team. Robeson, who had grown to be a considerable 6'2" and 190 pounds, nevertheless incurred numerous injuries, including a broken nose, a smashed hand, and a dislocated shoulder, none of which can be summarily chalked up to happenstance. But while he was disheartened, if not infuriated, over this initial experience, Robeson's father and brother would not let him quit. Accordingly, then, after ten days of recuperation, Robeson was back on the field but with a decidedly more prickly determination.

Robeson would later recall his ordeal by fire in an interview with *New York Times* reporter Robert Van Gelder. He admitted to rage, a rage to kill, even going so far as to lift a tough young running back named Kelly above his head for a bone-crushing tackle only to be deterred by the Rutgers coach who quickly blew the whistle to prevent serious injury and likely even more serious repercussions. Robeson had made the team and would become its star, but he would pay the price typically afforded a black man trying to make it in a white man's world.[7]

As a telling aside, former teammates would long differ on whether Robeson was deliberately subjected to a brutal hazing during these early scrimmages, but Robeson's skills as a football player were never in doubt. Periodic reports often extolled Robeson's versatility and excellence, which must have come as something of a shock to both teammates and coaches alike given the times. Regardless, he played many positions on both offense and defense—all brilliantly and in many ways presaging future developments within the game. For example, Robeson developed into the prototypical tight end who could block proficiently and turn short passes into long yardage while bowling over would-be tacklers. As a roving defender, he helped establish the role of what is today the middle linebacker. Furthermore, observers marveled at Robeson's brilliance, but they would also note an edginess to his performances that belied a boiling resentment borne of the mistreatment he had endured in his young life. Still, football alone would not define Robeson's collegiate experiences.[8]

In addition to his aforementioned athletic letters and All-American honors, Robeson's remarkably successful undergraduate years included his being named class valedictorian while gaining membership in Phi Beta Kappa.[9] With such impressive academic credentials, Robeson attempted to put sports behind him, but it would prove to be a struggle. Though he was admitted to Columbia Law School, Robeson, in order to defray law school tuition, also served as an assistant coach under Fritz Pollard, a future National Football League (NFL) Hall-of-Fame inductee, at nearby Lincoln University in Pennsylvania. While his involvement with the inimitable Pollard proved to be rewarding, it also forced Robeson to compromise, or at least put on hold, his loftier aspirations.[10]

In part through his association with Pollard, Robeson would go on to play professional football before the infamous ban on black players was imposed in 1934. Largely ignored then, professional football did not keep records, so it is difficult at best to judge Robeson's postgraduate performance. We do know, however, that alongside the legendary Pollard, who endured many similar indignities as the lone black player on the Brown University team some years prior, they were serious competitors facing a very serious combination of hard play and racially motivated retribution, though each would individually establish his own place in the precursor to what would become the NFL.[11] Robeson and Pollard individually and in tandem also demonstrated that they were the equal of anyone else, holding their own in integrated games while leading an all-black team, for example, to a stunning as well as unprecedented victory over an all-white all-star team in 1922,[12] but always within the contours of race.

Indeed, and in many ways in spite of his success, reports of Robeson's exploits were generally couched in the more predictably embedded racialized hyperbole of the day. He could be a "Dusky Rover" winding his way across the gridiron and even a "Football Othello,"[13] ironically enough, who towered above his contemporaries. In this regard, what he never appeared to be in any period accounts is a man, an athlete, or even a scholar sans the more prominent, some might say conventional, adjectives. What is equally apparent is that these experiences would help shape Robeson's consciousness in ways that would later pierce the American cultural veil in places well beyond the sporting milieu. Thus, while he was continually pushed to the margins by the prevailing sentiments of the day, and in spite of the odds against him, Robeson would manage to leave his mark on the athletic fields, though in hindsight one can see that sports were merely a springboard for a much more dynamic and decidedly versatile legacy.

ROBESON'S ATHLETIC CAREER IN CONTEXT

Obscured as Robeson's athletic legacy has become these many years removed, many Robeson scholars agree that Robeson played a central role in terms of laying something of a foundation for access to Jim Crow sports that would manifest itself decades later with Jackie Robinson in baseball, Kenny Washington and Woody Strode in football, and Chuck Cooper in basketball and the others that would follow in their footsteps.[14] In his assessment of Robeson's athletic career, for example, sociologist Harry Edwards observes that Robeson won respect from opposing coaches with his fierce play in spite of the prevailing racial climate that forced him to observe the indignities of the muted form of Jim Crow often at work in the North.[15] That Robeson was able to turn heads is in this regard significant in its own right, especially given the extraordinary obstacles placed in his path. He was most assuredly a man in a particularly challenging context, one that maintained that as a black man in a white world, he was expected to adhere to certain measures of propriety and convention, though for someone as proud and certainly as erudite as Robeson, this must have been intolerable on the best of days.

Indeed, while there is little hard evidence to suggest that he openly protested his treatment at the hands of predominantly white and predatory forces during his developmental years, he nevertheless seemed resigned to redressing on- and off-field slights with a matched aggression that offered a glimpse of the uncompromising nature he would later display as he matured, which seems quite similar to the transformation we would later see in Jackie Robinson once Branch Rickey lifted Robinson's prohibition on fighting back after the 1949 season. In contrast to Robinson, however, who took a more overtly physical stand against prejudice, fighting and scowling his way through the remainder of his playing days, Robeson seems to have channeled his anger and his angst into his many off-field pursuits. In this regard, Robeson had developed a sort of bipolar bearing toward a conspicuously bipolar world, though not every critic sees Robeson's athletic exploits in this particular context.

In his examination of 1930s America, Murray Kempton offers a less generous appraisal of Robeson's career trajectory relative to his links to American racial policy. Virtually bypassing Robeson's playing days and all that they would encompass, Kempton compares Paul Robeson's later exploits overseas to those of Blues singer Bessie Smith and union leaders Thomas Patterson and A. Philip Randolph. In this regard, Kempton can claim that Robeson—similarly—escaped from the horrors of racism inflicted upon American blacks through his celebrity. Observing this principally through Robeson's decision to move abroad after his playing days, Kempton claims that an expatriate's life in Europe constituted what Kempton would deem an avoidance adaptation, and, thus, because Robeson was so lionized in Europe, he did not in turn have to shoulder the awful burden of race as he would in America.[16]

Yet even Kempton has to concede that the young, pre-celebrity Robeson, continually facing Jim Crow in its myriad forms, could be uniquely prepared for such responses by virtue of his emergent athletic stature, which is clearly demonstrated by rival players (and some teammates), who had grown accustomed to reminding him through patterns of concentrated violence and those recurring social affronts that he was, at the end of the day, still a Negro in spite of his success. Thus, while some might argue that Robeson's relatively controlled demeanor on such occasions was a model for any marginalized sportsman (again, think of Jackie Robinson's non-aggression pact with Branch Rickey) but a step back in terms of the fight for social justice, Robeson's position as an African American meant that without recourse he had little choice but to toe whatever lines that might be available to him. His behavior, then, is not borne of the sort of fearfulness or avoidance that Kempton assumes. Rather, it is informed by a recognition that racial lines drawn had to be observed if not tolerated, making his actions less a matter of apprehension or even uncertainty and, rather, a more calculated and tactical retreat with a few timely retaliatory shots thrown in for good measure!

On this issue of retribution, Robeson would recall his football days later in his life and report with some muted satisfaction that there had been moments when he found it gratifying to retaliate in the middle of some of those raucous pile-ups. Certainly, football with its sanctioned violence offers such moments even for the most put-upon participant. Given that Robeson's game, unlike that of the speedier and more elusive Fritz Pollard, was one that relied upon the rarified combination of power and intellect, it stands to reason that Robeson was in a unique position to exact some degree of physical payback, something that later black stars such as Marian Motley and Jim Brown, who similarly learned to take as well as dole out punishment, would have to learn during their storied careers. In this regard, Robeson's ability to stick with it is as much a testament to his extraordinarily high threshold for pain and resolve as it is to the insistent prodding by both his father and brother. As he himself would one day acknowledge, "Sports was an important part of my life in those days,"[17] which seems to make the underestimation of Robeson's athletic legacy all the more puzzling.

It is imperative as well to recall once again the historical context with which Robeson arrived at his athletic prime. In this most confounding age, Robeson demonstrated a remarkable degree of grace under pressure, the hallmark of the Hemingway hero, something that was very much on display throughout his life. Moreover, in his successful pursuit of athletic glory, Robeson debunked the widely held belief that blacks were inferior, at least athletically, and in the process, as historian Lamont Yeakey contends, Robeson broadened the humanity of whites, albeit in a physical context, and often without even realizing it.[18]

Robeson appears to have taken his athletic ability in stride, recognizing that at best it was a way to survive and at the least it was a means to a much larger end. As is often the case with talented athletes who skirt the traditional All-American image by presenting something other than the Anglo-Saxon masculine ideal, i.e. Jim Thorpe, Hank Greenberg, Roberto Clemente, Robeson could deliver but rarely satisfy. So, for example, when he would be offered thousands of dollars to fully commit to professional sports—boxing as well as football—Robeson typically spurned both as corrupting and alien, preferring instead to study the law, though finances (and racism) at times would force his hand as discussed above.[19] Moreover, when the press lauded his talents and rued his graduation, Robeson responded: "Negro prejudice has two sides. When people hate you, they go a little crazy. But when they like you, they go a little crazy too. In football days, I got more praise than I deserved."[20] This sort of response might have seemed at the least curious to fans and teammates alike, but in retrospect it appears to incorporate the lot of those caught in the middle of this most debilitating tug-of-war. But it was also a game that Robeson was forced to play throughout the various stages of his life both in and out of the sporting spotlight, one that contributed a great deal to the public persona he gradually built for himself as well as that which was being constructed around him.

AN ICONIC FIGURE

The forces that often drove Robeson to be heroic on the field and off, to honor his name and his race, and to become a popular campus and national success story, meshed remarkably well in the Rutgers environment in spite of the social and political climates of the day. On the one hand, Robeson was quickly becoming a bonafide black American hero who had prevailed over the racialized climate that so defined America. On the other hand, he could be viewed as a white American icon because he was a football star and even academic model for students and faculty alike at Rutgers College, a John Henry figure for his time who could both charm the masses while staying true to his nature and his own people.[21]

His success symbolized the so-deemed *talented tenth* segregation of the early twentieth century, a system in which a few exceptional black men and women would be afforded a proper education in segregated institutions of higher education while millions of others were summarily excluded. This success and his acceptance at Rutgers also narrated a larger American myth—that everybody can make it in America, and that the son of a slave can grow up to become valedictorian at Rutgers College.

In spite of what was unfolding before him, Robeson entered his postcollegiate life with a great deal of optimism about America. In his senior thesis he argued that with the passage of the Fourteenth Amendment, the Constitution was finally made whole, finally rendered a just document because it finally defined citizenship in a way that made the travesty of the Dred Scott decision no longer possible while opening the door for bestowing citizenship rights on all Americans.

In his 1919 valedictory speech, "The New Idealism," he proffered an optimistic vision for a new post–World War I generation of African Americans who by then realized that their success lay in their own hands and not in white America's. His performance inserted one caveat: white America would have to meet its black citizenry halfway. That he would later demonstrate a willingness to sacrifice all of his success to protest against America's post–World War II failings was directly related to the sort of idealism he displayed at such a relatively young age, but it also goes to demonstrate the extent to which Robeson believed in the idea of America in spite of what he must surely had known would be a costly if not Pyrrhic battle.

A bewildered contemporary of Robeson's at Rutgers, a white man, in the aftermath of Robeson's very public fall would later recall that on the occasion of his valedictory speech, Robeson had the entire nation in his hands and could have done anything and become anything he wanted. This, however, would be a lament issued while the speaker was securely entrenched in 1949 when he could not understand why Robeson would have turned on America and declared that blacks would not fight for America against the Soviet Union. Regardless of this spectator's' lament, he had unwittingly stumbled onto a connection. Robeson's meteoric and very public rise and subsequent fall linked Robeson's powerful optimism for the idea behind America, that every person can rise to his or her level through ability and opportunity, to his later rejection of unswerving loyalty to America. What was omitted in this account, thus, is the toll that segregation, disfranchisement, and discrimination takes alongside of those daily reminders that are in place to thwart the lofty goals and aspirations for those pushed to the edge.[22]

For some, this seeming contradiction between the American idea of inclusion and the American practice of exclusion and exploitation did not burn as hotly as in Robeson. There were certainly cynics in both camps who never believed in America anyway. Robeson believed all the rhetoric behind the American Dream, believed, *a la* Booker T. Washington, that one could rise in America to the limit of one's bootstraps; that merit would be recognized in America; and, most importantly, that any migrant could come to America from anywhere and become an American, a respected citizen of this country and an integral part of *American-ness* in a way that was not true in any other country. Thus, the idealism expressed in Robeson's speech epitomized the optimistic vision of the Enlightenment cast over an entire generation of young so-called New Negro intellectuals, writers, and artists who would create the literature and art of the Harlem Renaissance in the 1920s.

What the aforementioned observer also failed to see embedded more discreetly in Robeson's earlier affirmations was the rage that he would later express when America's promises were not kept. In turn, that rage would be best articulated in the summer of that same year by those other New Negroes, the largely Southern-born working class of like-minded idealistic African Americans that came to Northern cities during World War I and were forced to endure segregated housing in addition to the beatings and the wholesale and wanton murder in the city streets of the once-vaunted North by whites in race riots such as in 1919. Former black sharecroppers and their allies fought back against these forces with a ferocity and viciousness that frightened their enemies, seeming to declare all the while that if America had no intentions of including its black citizenry, then its black citizenry would just as soon tear it down. In that sense, Robeson's anger (and that of others of his generation) shows how powerful and dangerous it was for a generation of African Americans to actually believe in the American credo. Such anger led directly to the kind of revolutionary rage that had inspired the Founding Fathers to overthrow their government because it was unwilling to live up to its own promise, an irony not lost then or now.

Those Harlem Renaissance–inspired ideas, that one can be black and successful without confining one's life to protest, helped Robeson be successful. He was also aided by the cultural changes of the period that saw him emerge at a time when dark skin color and being black and proud and its resulting identification with Africa and with the folk of the African American community was in ascendance in American cultural life. But it is through these experiences, believing in the transformative ability to change American racial relations, that Robeson received an education that others, and especially those who were not in the (white) public eye, did not experience. Thus, as Robeson attempted to act out his own social project, he came to realize that the problems of representation as a black man typically boiled down to being owned by the means of cultural production.

THE REPRESENTATION CONUNDRUM

To be sure, Robeson struggled with the issue of representation throughout his life—namely how he and other marginalized people were depicted and ultimately commodified in and by the media. He began to question his value as an artist when he observed how his image was often manipulated on the stage and in the movies. At a time when most African American actors, for example, simply regurgitated stereotypical roles in Hollywood movies, Robeson, emboldened by his celebrity, openly criticized the inherently racist imagery in films and eventually refused to act in American movies, going so far as to force the 1940 tour of the play *John Henry* to open in New York rather than perform the title role before a segregated audience in Washington DC.

Equally as problematic for Robeson and the American authorities both was his drift toward socialism and his alliance with the Stalinists. Extraordinarily popular, he was no mere State Department wonk nor was he a nondescript leftist face in the crowd, the sort of nightmare scenario that posed all sorts of dilemmas for an increasingly intransigent state. Nonetheless, Robeson became the symbol of resistance against the House on Un-American Activities (HUAC) Committee during the peak years of the anti-Communist era and referred to its members as if they were the embodiment of betrayal, the ramifications of which can be found in the pace with which his fall became fodder for a reactionary and complicit media that seemed ready to pounce on any opportunity to debase his reputation.[23]

Many since have pondered Robeson's ultimate goals and objectives in regard to his very public fall, which has led to a wealth of speculation and such. Many of these same voices—black and white—tend toward a more psychological approach toward making sense of his activism, intimating that ultimately he buckled under the weight of oppression and his role as a public force for change. For example, in his acclaimed biography of Robeson, Martin Duberman suggests that Robeson privately bemoaned or lamented the fact that a white woman who had promised to marry him during the 1930s abandoned him, a disappointment that showed up in his dealings with other women in his life.[24]

Duberman similarly unfurls a much more graphic depiction of the extent to which the public Robeson was forced to endure a string of indignities. For example, during the 1949 wedding of his son, Paul Jr., the wedding party was faced with a rerun of an earlier scene that involved reporters crowding around for statements, onlookers taunting bride and groom, photographers poking cameras in their faces, and the rowdy inquisitive public who came to witness the private marriage ceremony of his son to Marilyn Paula Greenberg. This private affair was disrupted by the media wanting to use the event to get Paul Robeson to talk about his "un-American" activities in Europe, though Robeson in his typically more feisty style responded with defiance and grace.[25] Furthermore, as Duberman informs us, that Paul Robeson was subjected to such disgraceful treatment as being routinely followed by FBI agents while having his mail intercepted, his phone conversations bugged, his public appearances monitored and reported, and, above all, always having to maintain a stance of opposition, contributed to building up a potentially explosive amount of anguish and rage in Paul Robeson, thus transforming him from a celebrity icon to an antiracist and anticapitalist hero.[26]

While incidents such as these would certainly come with their own private pain, it is doubtful that such a monumental life change can be explained by select isolated personal experiences, especially when juxtaposed to the many challenges Robeson faced much earlier in his life. At most, however, these incidents, and many others, serve to highlight a much more telling matter: the kinds of freedoms Robeson was alleged to have enjoyed as an international icon were in fact illusory. In that sense, the illusion would, thus, attach itself to a deeper, longer termed process of emerging self-consciousness regarding his own limitations as a black artist while demonstrating that his future as a heroic figure was always in jeopardy. Still, it is never really clear that Robeson was being driven by psychosocial pressures as much as he was the force driving the discussions of what true liberation and freedom could mean for those on the outside of contemporary society. Moreover, and as he would demonstrate time and again, his was not the only future that consumed him, lending further credence to the notion that psychology alone was not at the forefront of his agenda.

Sometime in the 1930s, while still a beloved public figure, Robeson recognized that he could not transform the racist representations of African peoples on stage and in motion pictures unless he undertook an activist struggle to transform the system of international capitalism and racism that sustained those representations. Robeson answered the hero's challenge by attacking the obvious obstacles to his success as an artist by tying it to the underlying degradations of the humanity of all African peoples.

Perhaps contrary to Kempton's statements above, Robeson could come to such an analysis because he was a heralded performing artist at a crucial moment in American cultural history when technological innovation transformed entertainment in America from a participatory to a consumer-driven venture. In this regard, Robeson was part of the transformation in American culture whereby the primacy in the culture moved beyond the manipulation of words to the manipulation of images.

As a performing artist he was more sensitive to and directly dependent upon the economics of cultural production in the motion picture, concert, and legitimate theater world than, for example, a historian like W. E. B. Du Bois, or a philosopher like Alain Locke. In the 1930s, that dependency opened Robeson's eyes to the ways in which he and his art were used to advance the racial and class agendas he so vehemently rejected. Therefore, when he shifted the emphasis of his public career from cultural production to the interrogation of the social formation that lay beneath it, Robeson risked the future of his career as an artist on the willingness of a politically conscious working class of all hues to support his heroic activism.[27]

Robeson's chief concern here was that the class-conscious basis for such activism, i.e., the willingness of white workers to join with black workers in a sustained attack on the capitalist system, was never strong in America and probably reached its peak in the late 1930s and early 1940s before evaporating during the anti-Communist campaigns of the postwar era. In this respect, government-led capitulation to anti-Communism destroyed Robeson's standing as one of the world's truly iconic figures just as the cosmopolitan experience of his international celebrity remade his identity on a more globalized basis. Moreover, the working- and middle-class Americans who were his natural audiences had not shared that experience, which would in the end serve to handcuff Robeson as a political leader as he challenged a resolutely obdurate American political oligarchy.

Robeson's confrontation with his cultural impotence would then drive his consciousness further as he began to split with his liberal pluralist politics to become an advocate of class struggle and the more radical critique of establishment culture. Robeson also remained a sponsor of what would be considered African American cultural pride, as signified by his lifelong performance of the spirituals in his concerts, his advocacy of African independence and self-rule, his interest in African affairs, and his definition of himself as an African. By becoming a member of the West African Students Association in London, for example, Robeson also realized that his individual choice as a black artist was limited by the range of possible options afforded him in a film industry that was a multinational capitalist institution.[28]

Moreover, Robeson began to appreciate that without some fundamental change in the worldwide economic structure that supported the film industry and racial practices in America, he could never find fulfillment as an artist. As such, he realized that identity is indeed socially constructed by others, and, accordingly, he accepted the notion that he must reveal and transform those social forces to achieve his freedom. In this regard, he would come to recognize, as Toni Cade Bambara would observe years later: "I do not think that literature [for Robeson substitute *artistic performance*] is the primary instrument for social transformation but I do think that literature [read *art*] has potency. So I work to celebrate struggle."[29] In taking on this mantle, Robeson entered the African American tradition of *truth telling* and of speaking the truth to power, matters that can be uncovered within contemporary debates that explore the coalescence of celebrity and political confrontation that are particularly revealing when juxtaposed to Robeson's own uniquely forthright yet evocative manner.

A MORE MODERN GLANCE

To be sure, Robeson had once enjoyed the sort of international celebrity that was reserved primarily for the likes of white Hollywood icons and professional baseball players, which alone makes him a most unique figure. With the exception of perhaps the American ex-patriot Josephine Baker, though she had at best a much more limited appeal, he was not only the best-known African American performing artist of his era; he was also one of the world's highest paid commercial artists. But unlike others caught up in the hustle and flow of the spotlight, Robeson never seemed to lose his proletarian sensibilities to the bright lights and transparent exhibitionism that often informs the celebrated life. Thus, in an attempt to add clarity in this regard, it might be helpful to offer some comparative analysis to the Robeson legacy by hitching it to the one contemporary celebrity who thus far has been able to achieve a fairly similar global trajectory, basketball's Michael Jordan.

Jordan is certainly a most intriguing figure. Omnipresent long after his playing days, he has nonetheless invited a degree of criticism that encompasses a range of comparatively minor personal gaffes and indiscretions, some of which are wholly out of his control but many of which can be linked directly to his varied business interests outside of basketball. Yet, if there is a theme in Jordan's legacy, it is his glaringly pervasive a-politicization, vestiges of which can be found in his myriad commercial endeavors.

Jordan's celebrity, which is often informed by these interests, has ostensibly turned him into a more nebulous and seemingly detached figure within an often contentious sporting climate. This can certainly work to his advantage in terms of the control and maintenance of his public persona, but it also has a tendency to put him at odds with contemporaries and history both. Indeed, even a subsequent generation of NBA stars seems to have lost any linkage to Jordan at all, as evidenced by Allen Iverson's now (in)famous observation "Jordan is not my hero. None of my heroes wear suits."[30]

In some ways Jordan's extraordinary rise, tied into the way that his character was carefully crafted for consumption, may indeed be indicative of the nature of celebrity in the twenty-first century. Unquestionably, the explosion of media and the speed with which information flows lends itself to the sort of spectacle that ultimately took a rather unassuming and very young collegiate phenom and turned him virtually overnight into the most adored brand name in sports history. Certainly the demands on his time and person and the sheer weight of responsibility that comes with his many corporate obligations would test the resolve of even the most centered individual. And clearly Jordan bears responsibility for his actions—or inactions, as the case may be—but, at the same time, that these obligations serve in turn to hold him to a standard of behavior unreserved for others is equally problematic.

It has thus become quite common to report that black athletes like Jordan and his generation of African American athletes born in the 1970s and 1980s have abdicated their responsibility to the community with an apathy that borders on treason. As William C. Rhoden explains in his *Forty Million Dollar Slaves: the Rise, Fall, and Redemption of the Black Athlete*, this is because for this generation of young black athletes, there is a disconnect between their own experiences and the experiences of those who came before them in terms of fighting for equality and social justice or taking a stand on the larger community's struggle for freedom against racism. According to Rhoden, then, for these young generations of African American athletes, the hunger to champion community values and be advocates for social justice causes are nonexistent ideals or projects to aim for in their purview. As a result, the concept that these generations of African American athletes belong to a larger community with a shared history is a hazy notion, if it exists at all, which, reverting back to the theme of this work, is a very un-Paul Robeson-like approach to the notion of social activism.[31]

Similarly, in Jordan's ubiquitous "Be Like Mike"[32] Gatorade campaign, we can find a similar thrust that seems to drive Jordan further away from a Robeson-like standard. This spot is intended to highlight Jordan's status as a role model and the embodiment of iconic values and elevated aspirations. However, implicit throughout is the idea that because Jordan plays basketball, is perhaps the best basketball player ever, and is a media and advertising industry darling, he is a hero—and a black hero at that. Yet Jordan's construction throughout this (and the many other promotional interests constructed around his image) also suggests something regarding the poignancy, or lack thereof, of his and other contemporary black athletes' position in American culture that is also vital to our understanding of Robeson's status as a modern American icon: that it exists on the best day as incredibly tenuous, a fragility best expressed in the antithesis of the "Be Like Mike" motif: "If I did not play sports, a spectacle for you, the consuming audience, would I be anything but another subhuman in the derogatory language of the American slavery era?"

This sort of query, ironically, could have been posed by Paul Robeson to the country in 1950 when it began to ban his records, cancel his concerts, remove his name from the list of All-Americans, and treat him like a nonperson: "If Paul Robeson ceases to play football, entertain you on the stage or on the screen, will he remain your hero?" The answer from the majority of Americans was no, but the answer from a significant minority of black Americans and a smaller percentage of white Americans, plus thousands of Europeans, Russians, and other nationals, was yes, and it continued to be yes in the 1960s and 1970s. Robeson became a hero for many people precisely because he was not in the modern lexicon Jordan-esque—a yes man for corporate America—but rather a challenge to the system that exploits African Americans for profit. Robeson was a hero because he stood up to the FBI, the State Department, and President Harry S. Truman's campaign to stop his criticism of American racial and human rights violations. The price he paid for that stand was enormous—his career, his health, and his peace of mind. In contrast, today's athletes seem so much less inclined to grasp the Robeson mantle and run with it accordingly. The financial stakes may be higher today, but the lasting effects of such a turn have the potential to resonate several generations forward.

TOWARD A MOST UNTIMELY DENOUEMENT

Paul Robeson's rise to stardom was certainly unprecedented given that during his lifetime, race played a central role in determining how much success a person could achieve. Accordingly, for an individual to be successful as Paul Robeson, an African American who hailed from a generation barely removed from American slavery, was an incredible feat, serving in many respects as a model of accomplishment.

By 1946, however, the strain of balancing his art and his vision for a better America began to tell on Robeson, as exemplified in his decision to stop performing in films and on the dramatic stage. He limited his concert singing as well, confining himself to a few singing engagements so that he could turn most of his energy towards his heroic quest of becoming a political activist to bring about a democratic and perhaps even multicultural America. In reality, however, it was not Robeson but the United States government that had ended the marriage for him. Despite his declining film and dramatic career, Robeson had remained such a powerful icon, such an international symbol of courage and accomplishment, that the United States felt he had to be brought down, had to be disciplined (in the language used by Michel Foucault in *Discipline and Punish*[33]) into another kind of symbol, a sign to others that if they too *stood up to the man* (in the narrative of slave resistance that the historian Eugene Genovese discusses in *Roll, Jordan, Roll*[34]), they too would be crushed.

Robeson's harassment and confinement, after his passport was taken from him in 1950 and before it was returned in 1958, constituted a system designed to connote to observers that the state has the power to control, to observe, to demean, and to humiliate whomever it wishes whenever it cares to, but the reality was far more complex. Unlike the official story of his destruction by the state, Robeson continued to lecture, to speak out, and to challenge the system that metaphorically imprisoned him and all those who spoke their minds in the 1950s.

Robeson was active during the early part of the decade as the still-standing hero who lectured to labor unions that would have him, colleges and universities whose student bodies wanted to hear him, and to smaller collections of progressive people, sometimes gathered around him in living rooms throughout America.[35] And yet, when his passport was returned, Robeson left the United States for Europe, where he was welcomed throughout the continent. He returned to the Soviet Union and to a hero's welcome and basked in the glory of someone who had stood up to imperial power and lived. But Robeson also had paid a terrible price during these years. Not only his physical but also his mental health was damaged beyond repair. He encountered, struggled with, and succumbed to depression and ultimately terminated his active speaking career after he returned to the United States in 1963.

Nevertheless, Robeson was not destroyed as a heroic figure. Part of the continuing attraction of Robeson is the way in which his story connects with universal narratives of the heroic. Like many an ancient Greek and Egyptian hero, Robeson had to leave home, had to go on a dangerous journey, only to return battered and bruised. He went off to Europe and the Soviet Union and experienced much as an icon that most Americans would not, and he returned to his homeland with scars, like a modern day Ulysses—wounded, bent, and battered but not bowed. Symbolically murdered as an American icon, Robeson was resurrected by those who revered him more as a hero.

AN EXTRAORDINARY LEGACY

In 1954, Rutgers University published a list of its sixty greatest football players. Conspicuously and absurdly absent was Paul Bustill Robeson. Sports Information Director William McKenzie called it "a conspiracy of silence."[36] Because his alma mater refused to sponsor him, the rejection of Robeson spilled over to the National Football Hall of Fame.[37]

A reversal of fortune, however, begins in 1970 when a committee of sports cognoscenti and Rutgers personnel, including Coach John Bateman, put his name in nomination. Rejected until August 25, 1995, the great athlete at long last entered his alma mater's Hall of Fame.[38] For Robeson, the union with football's elite came too little, too late. For the faithful, however, this delayed honor proved author Leo Tolstoy correct in his profound observation that "God sees the truth—but waits."[39]

In the final analysis, when football functioned as the moral equivalent of war, what did this noble warrior accomplish along the banks of New Jersey's Raritan River? True, segregation did not vanish during his glory years. Nor could Robeson strike a fatal blow against segregation away from the battlefields of sports. Thanks to his presence, however, black participation in a once totally white intercollegiate environment measurably improved while public appreciation of black talent also increased, markedly. As Professor Jeffrey Stewart astutely observes, Robeson's body became the subject of riveting attention, while at the same time, his intellectual accomplishments grew to be the object of awe.[40]

In a cache of photographs recently discovered, the portrayal of Robeson in the nude may have contributed to a profound insight ensuing from the Harlem Renaissance in which Paul Robeson played an integral part—namely that black is beautiful. This extraordinarily athletic Apollo was the epitome of black beauty.[41]

There is, alas, also one disturbing afterthought. Robeson's account of his football experience is almost too sweet in self-denial. He must have harbored deep rage within, which, when unleashed, caused the fire in his soul to burn incessantly. The oxygen of other atmospheres—such as the Soviet Union and Eastern Europe, where he was lionized, admired, and loved—fed his anger at America. But despite his support of Communism, we must not extenuate or distort the injustice visited on this great man. We must also remember that Robeson's heroic entry into the deep river of American life coincided with his immersion—let's call it baptism—in sports but—as always—constructed in such a way as to make palatable the thoughts and actions of a black man in a white world not quite prepared to hear what he had to say.

Nevertheless, Robeson's reentry into the cultural landscape of the very country that hastened his demise marks a fascinating reinterpretation of the Robeson saga. Still, it would appear that the cultural clash that continues to dominate modern headlines serves often to render the whole of the discussion of the nature of athletes and community and activism rather banal and well beyond the point. Robeson was, to be sure, a most exceptional being, but to hold others to his standard of exception is both dangerous and ill conceived. Moreover, it shows a much deeper capacity for retarding the very measures for change that Robeson himself fought so hard and sacrificed so much to achieve.

He may have come out of his trial unbroken, unbent, and repositioned, and his story may have taken on an entirely new dimension in many of the very sectors of society that had once rejected him outright. Still, it is important that successive generations think of him not as a model but as a man. Otherwise, the temptation to take his legacy out of its historical context stands poised to render obsolete those whose voices and actions are truly capable of injecting the spirit of Robeson into an era that needs as many Paul Robesons as it can conceivably generate.

NOTES

1. See, for example, C. Keith Harrison and Brian Lampman, "The Image of Paul Robeson: Role Model for the Student and Athlete," *Rethinking History* 5, no.1, (2001): 118–20, and Joseph Dorinson, "Athletes and Activism at Armegeddon," *Pennsylvania History*. 66, no. 1 (Winter 1999): 17.

2. Lou Little, *Lou Little Papers 1910–1977* (New York: Columbia University, Manuscript Collection and Rare Books).

3. Dorinson, "Athletes and Activisim," 23.

4. Joseph Dorinson, "Something to Cheer About: Paul Robeson, Athlete" in *Paul Robeson: Essays on His Life and Legacy*, eds. Joseph Dorinson and William Pencak (Jefferson, NC: McFarland and Company, 2002), 68.

5. Paul Robeson, *Here I Stand*. (New York: Othello Associates, 1958), 22.

6. Lloyd Brown, *The Young Paul Robeson* (Boulder, CO: Westview Press, 1997), 46.

7. Brown, *The Young Paul Robeson*, 62. See also William C. Rhoden, *Forty Million Dollar Slaves: The Rise, Fall, and Redemption of the Black Athlete* (New York: Crown Publishers, 2006), 15–16, and Harrison and Lampman, "The Image," 118–21.

8. Dorinson, "Something to Cheer About," 69.

9. Dorinson, "Athletes and Activisim," 17.

10. See Harrison and Lampman, "The Image," 120.

11. Joe Powers, Sr. and Mark Rogovin, *Paul Robeson Rediscovered: An Annotated Listing of His Chicago History from 1921–1958* (Chicago: Columbia College Paul Robeson 100th Birthday Committee, 2000), 7.

12. Powers and Rogovin, *Paul Robeson Rediscovered*, 313, 711.

13. Lenwood G. Davis, *A Paul Robeson Research Guide: A Selective Annotated Bibliography* (Westport, CT: Greenwood Press, 1982), 7.

14. These individuals are credited with having reintegrated the big three of American professional sports in the post–World War II era.

15. Harry Edwards, *Sociology of Sport* (Homewood, IL: Dorsey Press, 1973), 109. Edwards goes on to report that due to his "radical outspokenness," Robeson's name was essentially wiped from the collegiate record books after 1950.

16. Murray Kempton, *Part of Our Time: Some Ruins and Monuments of the Thirties* (New York: Simon and Schuster, 1955), 233–38.

17. Davis, *A Paul Robeson Research Guide,* 67.

18. Lamont Yeakey, "The Early Years of Paul Robeson: Prelude to the Making of a Revolutionary" (master's thesis, Columbia University, 1971), 53.

19. Yeakey, "The Early Years," 56.

20. Yeakey, "The Early Years," 40.

21. For a more thorough description of the John Henry legend, see, for example, Lawrence Levine, *Black Culture and Black Consciousness: Afro-American Folk Thought from Slavery to Freedom* (London: Oxford University Press, 1977), 420–27. Suffice it to say, however, that at least prior to his public demise, Robeson and Joe Louis come as close to embodying the John Henry mystique as any other African Americans.

22. Jeffrey Stewart, "Paul Robeson: The Icon" in *Paul Robeson: Essays on His Life and Legacy*, eds. Joseph Dorinson and William Pencak, (Jefferson, NC: McFarland and Company, 2002), 206.

23. Stewart, "Paul Robeson: the Icon," 195.

24. Martin Duberman, *Paul Robeson: A Biography* (New York: New Press, 1988), 294, 614, 312–13, 676.

25. Duberman, *Paul Robeson: A Biography*, 356.

26. Duberman, *Paul Robeson: A Biography*, 432, 693.

27. Stewart, "Paul Robeson: The Icon," 195.

28. Duberman, *Paul Robeson: A Biography*, 628. See also Stewart, "Paul Robeson: The Icon," 208, and Hakim Adi, *West Africans in Britain: 1900–1960 Nationalism, Pan-Africanism and Communism* (London: Lawrence & Wishart, 1998), 41, 63, 78.

29. Toni C. Bambara, "Toni Cade Bambara," in *Black Women Writers at Work*, ed. Claudia Tate, (New York: Continuum Press, 1983), 18.

30. Dave Zirin, "Budweiser's Racist Commercial: What's the Matter with 'Leon'?" *CounterPunch*, 1 December 2004 http://www.counterpunch.org/zirin12012004.htm (24 July 2007).

31. Rhoden, *Slaves*, 200.

32. See Darren Rovell, "Be Like Mike," *Authors Review Online*, 2005 http://www.authoreview.com/authors/Rovell.obd.htm (24 July 2007). Rovell reports that Gatorade televised its first "Be Like Mike" commercial on 24 July 1991. See also Darren Rovell, *First in Thirst: How Gatorade Turned the Science of Sweat into a Cultural Phenomenon* (New York: American Management Association, 2005).

33. Michael Foucault, *Discipline and Punish: The Birth of the Prison* (New York: Vintage Press, 1995).

34. Eugene D. Genovese, *Roll, Jordan, Roll: The World the Slaves Made* (New York: Vintage, 1976), 587–98.

35. See Mary Cygan, "A Man of His Times: Paul Robeson and the Press, 1924–1976," *Pennsylvania History* 66, no. 1 (1999): 39–40.

36. In Dorinson, "Something to Cheer About," 73.

37. Duberman, *Paul Robeson: A Biography*, 760.

38. Francis C. Harris, "Paul Robeson" in *Paul Robeson: Artist and Citizen*, ed. Jeffrey Stewart, (New Brunswick, NJ: Rutgers University Press, 1998), 45.

39. Leo Tolstoy, *God Sees the Truth, But Waits* (Mankato, MN: Creative Education, Classic Short Stories, 1986).

40. Jeffrey Stewart, "The Black Body: Robeson as a Work of Art and Politics," in *Paul Robeson: Artist and Citizen*, ed. Jeffrey Stewart, (New Brunswick, NJ: Rutgers University Press, 1998), 135–63.

41. Stewart, "The Black Body," 135.

REMAKING AN OVERLOOKED ICON

The Reconstruction of Jim Thorpe

ROBERT W. REISING

INTRODUCTION

Born in the turbulent 1960s, both Bo Jackson and Deion Sanders took advantage of pre-professional baseball and football success as well as dispositions that attracted and valued media hype to become national celebrities—almost cult figures—on whom the sports spotlight could never shine brightly and frequently enough. Pocketing millions because of their athletic talents and no less for their endorsements and public appearances, this dynamic duo set a standard for public adulation that will be difficult, indeed, to match. "Bo Knows," as the commercial loop reminded us,[1] is unmistakably tied to Jackson, as is a persona that his promoters would have the world believe possesses knowledge and talents unavailable to ordinary humans, or even to the universe's finest intellects. Similarly, "Neon Deion" and "Prime Time" are inseparable from Sanders, whose feats and celebrations in sports arenas communicate that he commands the athletically inconceivable. Jackson and Sanders both loom as icons that technology, temperament, and fan mania have elevated to Herculean heights inaccessible to other mortals.

Yet neither of these two athletes, talented though they were, deserves to claim a greatness unseen in the past. As Dave Kindred, the gifted sportswriter, has accurately decreed, contemporary sports aficionados possess but a five-minute memory, one that leaves any achievement or performer in the historically distant at best a blur, a vague, indiscernible entity the particulars of whom have long ago disappeared from mind and recollection. The immediate occupies every corner and crevice of the contemporary brain, Kindred argues, and, therefore, when mentioned, heroics and heroes of yesteryear elicit blank stares or a moronic "Huh?"[2] While in the current decade, Jackson and Sanders may be hazily recalled, Jim Thorpe can seldom claim such a distinction. Yet in Thorpe, Jackson and Sanders had at least their athletic equal.

Thorpe was in every respect a sports marvel whose exploits of the first three decades of the twentieth century were tarnished by Machiavellian maneuvers designed to save from disgrace humans of far less integrity. He was the quintessential and proverbial "fall guy," a Native American who lived and performed in an era vastly different from that in which Sanders and Jackson—also persons of color—have gained fame and fortune.

During the years in which Thorpe mesmerized all who witnessed his performances, Caucasians alone were acceptable for sports success; a ward of the United States Government simply did not qualify. As such, as a Native American born in a nondescript cabin in Oklahoma Indian Territory in 1887, he was an unlikely candidate for international admiration, or even national respect.

NATIVE ATHLETE IN A WHITE MAN'S WORLD

The world that shaped Thorpe, it must be stressed, was vastly different from the world that celebrates him today. The Indian Territory of his birth and first years introduced him not to the complexities and contradictions of national and international athletic competition but to the satisfactions and challenges of the out-of-doors as well as to the demands and drudgery of tribal homesteading in late nineteenth-century America. The mindset and imprint of his Sac and Fox upbringing prepared him for a life that was to contrast dramatically with what he encountered on and after February 1, 1904, when, at the age of sixteen, he enrolled at the Carlisle Indian Industrial School in Carlisle, Pennsylvania.

It was at the Industrial School that Thorpe was to immerse himself in the priorities and mandates that were, first, to catapult him to unprecedented acclaim, later to plunge him into scandal and ignominy, and, finally, to restore him to a respect and adulation that few humans, in the world of sports or elsewhere, can claim in the new millennium. Throughout its thirty-nine year existence, this government-funded institution, founded by Richard Henry Pratt, a well-intentioned but badly misguided United States military officer, represented all that America believed important as it advanced westward while proclaiming race, ethnicity, and class the avenues to acceptance, opportunity, and influence. And it would be during Thorpe's two stints at Carlisle that the man who would become both heralded and reviled as the most spectacular athlete of his generation would find a marked degree of passable—if not downright aloof—nurturing.

Muscular Christianity dominated the nation's psyche for roughly four decades, 1880 to 1920, the period that saw Thorpe, like Carlisle, earn accolades that were but a prelude to embarrassment and discredit. While both Thorpe's muscle and the trappings of American-imbued Christianity emerged at the Pennsylvania institution, neither was tied to what G. Stanley Hall and other elitist intellectuals viewed as no less essential: the Caucasian Anglicanism of the Northeast. The fate and future of the nation, the pioneer psychologist and his followers maintained, rested with white Anglo-Saxon Protestants whose American roots lay not in the Middle

West but in New England. Physically, Thorpe qualified, but racially and religiously he was anything but ideal. As a teenager born and raised in Indian Territory who, at least nominally, claimed Roman Catholicism, he was only slightly more admirable than the African Americans whose forbears had arrived on this continent in chains and the immigrant hordes who, piling into America's blighted urban neighborhoods, were supposedly incapable of any ventures divorced from alcoholism, rowdyism, and ignorance.

In a sense, by the standards of Muscular Christianity, Thorpe was doubly cursed when entering Carlisle. By his own admission only five-eighths Indian, he also carried an abundance of Irish blood in his veins because of his grandfather on his paternal side, Hiram G. Thorpe, whose forbears proudly acknowledged ties to the Emerald Isle. To be legally a Native American was disadvantage enough in 1904; to carry both an Irish ancestry and an Irish name, as well, was a two-yoke burden for a youngster embarking on a five-year venture into Americanization.

Yet still other disadvantages accompanied young Thorpe into the school. One, fortunately, he literally outgrew. As he approached his seventeenth birthday, he was hardly an eye-catching physical specimen. At 5 feet, 5 $^1/_2$ inches tall and 115 pounds, he was but a shadow of the muscular speedster who was subsequently to grab headline upon headline across the globe. Admittedly, he was agile and graceful, assets that had served him well in athletics in Indian Territory, especially baseball; yet, initially at Carlisle, his height and weight denied him every opportunity at excellence in physical activities demanding bulk and power.

He was soon, too, to be disadvantaged in a far more significant way. The loss of his father, Hiram P. Thorpe, on April 22, 1904—less than three months after his enrollment—not only plunged the teenager into profound grief but deprived him of the last family member to whom he felt close. The victim of septicemia, a form of blood poisoning, while on a hunting expedition, Jim Thorpe's burly, brawling parent had hardly proven to be lovable and sensitive in his handling of his spirited offspring. Yet the pair carried a seldom-voiced respect for each other, and, hence, when news of Hiram P.'s passing reached the Industrial School, the younger Thorpe was submerged in sadness. He had lost his beloved twin brother, his inseparable companion, Charlie, in May of 1896, and his mother, a devout Roman Catholic, five years later. With the passing of his father, he was left without a family member to whom he could intimately and meaningfully relate. Emotionally as well as legally, he was an orphan, and the loneliness brought sorrow to his every fiber and lingered in his being when, three months later, Pratt, once-labeled "The Red Man's Moses,"[3] relinquished the leadership of Carlisle.

On June 15, 1904, Pratt was relieved of his duties as superintendent of the institution he had founded, an action whose full impact Thorpe was not to feel for almost a decade. Despite his shortcomings, Pratt had refused to view the Indian as inferior to the Caucasian and hence had championed total assimilation rather than the separate-but-equal perceptions and policies that his successors were quick to espouse. Thus, in this regard, while traps abounded for Thorpe throughout his stay at Carlisle, Pratt had been the one constant in his otherwise problematic and certainly complicated environment. Without Pratt, Thorpe became, predictably, even further set adrift by circumstance.

Clearly, neither of his successors was a Pratt—not in idealism, not in commitment, not in enthusiasm, not in integrity. Instead, William A. Mercer and Moses Friedman governed an institution indifferent to accountability, financial and otherwise, and were blind to curricular and extracurricular demands that would allow its students to realize and exploit the potential Pratt had so vigorously refused to deny or denigrate. A sports enthusiast, less than three years into his superintendency, Mercer rehired as football coach Glenn Scobey "Pop" Warner, the man who had frequently clashed with Pratt over recruiting tactics during Warner's initial stay at Carlisle.

ENTER "POP" WARNER

When Warner, a self-serving opportunist whom Thorpe's roommate, Gus Welch, once publicly described as "a man with no principle,"[4] returned, he would discern that Thorpe was adding height, weight, and muscle to his diminutive frame. Conditions would find, however, that Warner, a talented lawyer whose genius as a sports innovator was exceeded only by his bent for the unethical and the unsavory, would also emerge as the orphan's surrogate parent, a father-figure unworthy of anyone's trust, least of all that of a Native American youngster as vulnerable and confused as he was honest, unsophisticated, and coordinated. Yet Thorpe did not immediately feel the influence of the coach who was forever to be linked with his athletic success.

Shortly after arriving at his new school, Thorpe entered the so-called "Outing System," a Pratt-introduced innovation that assigned Indian youngsters to off-campus Caucasian-overseen apprenticeships.[5] Silent and unresponsive because of the trio of deaths agonizing his head and heart, Thorpe was ideal, Mercer believed, for labors demanding movement rather than mind, energy not intellect. Two days after Pratt's dismissal as superintendent, and only weeks after Warner announced he was leaving Carlisle for the first time, Thorpe fell under the supervision of Mr. A. E. Buckholz of Somerton, Pennsylvania, for whom he prepared meals and kept house. Thus at the very time Thorpe was coming to detest domestic chores typically reserved for nonwhites, Warner was honing his skills as football strategist at Cornell, where alcohol-filled alumni commonly demanded that the gridiron game be played their way, not the coach's.

Thorpe's similarly troubled sojourn lasted less than a year before Carlisle's work-release program moved him into a pair of often-interrupted assignments that provided him with no greater tranquility or stability, the first as a gardener in another Pennsylvania town, Dolington, the second as a farm foreman in Robbinsville,

New Jersey. Hence, by the time Warner had gratefully, if not graciously, exited Cornell and rushed to accept Mercer's invitation to return to Carlisle, Thorpe occupied less-than-prestigious campus quarters, what journalist Bill Crawford terms "the cold, damp, century-old guardhouse."[6] While farm work and New Jersey had brought strength and bulk to Thorpe's physical frame, it had done little to harness the demons that churned within that frame. Moreover, his bent for running from the distasteful or demeaning would continue three years into his Carlisle matriculation, combining with the anguish capped by his father's unexpected and premature passing, which would conspire to render the soon-to-be twenty-year-old erratic and disobedient.

Eventually time might well have brought Thorpe greater insight into and acceptance of life's inexplicable cruelties, but there was no need for it. While he never in his almost sixty-six years abandoned either his charismatic, carefree, competitive disposition or his refusal to tolerate indignities or insults, immediately ahead lay unanticipated ventures and human interactions that intrigued him. The timing was perfect. "Pop," with his exploitative, ingratiating ways, insinuated himself into his life and forced it into a 180-degree turn that, within a decade, catapulted Thorpe into international phenomenon and celebrity.

Indeed, it is likely that no other athletically inclined teenager ever unknowingly hungered more for acceptable activity and direction than did Thorpe in the spring of 1907. Almost 5 feet, 10 inches tall and 150 pounds, he subconsciously longed for a mentor whose guidance and sports savvy could graduate him from self-destructive behaviors to self-satisfying ones. Warner was that mentor. He was physically like Hiram P., athletically just as adept, and educationally all that Thorpe's deceased parent might have been had the latter been born into a more mainstreamed and privileged circumstance. Warner, however, possessed a gift that neither Hiram P. nor his son ever acquired or admired. He could be chameleonlike, capable of ingratiating himself with humans of every stripe.

Sincerity yielded to expediency in his interactions with both the wealthy and the lowly, especially the latter. In fact, Arthur Martin, once the Carlisle Athletic Department's secretary, proved himself a master of understatement when he once termed his administrative superior "quite an amateur psychologist."[7] Clearly, Warner was uncommon and uncanny in his interpersonal skills. Profanity, for example, flowed from his lips when it served his purposes but disappeared when it did not. Once he learned that Indian youth rarely responded positively when it reached their ears, he seldom called upon it in their presence. Warner lived for results. Ends justified means, in his belief system; pragmatism reigned over principle, as Welch's comment suggests.

With Pratt gone, Warner burgeoned into an icon—first at Carlisle and later across the continent. His effectiveness as a coach of track and field as well as of football won the admiration of every sports enthusiast in America. Overseen by Mercer and Friedman, he became his own supervisor, leading Carlisle to unprecedented success while simultaneously heaping largesse upon his athletic boys, saying that they were special and different from the rest of the student body. Predictably, that largesse also endeared "Pop" to the young men who were its recipients, Thorpe among them. Good living, in this regard, became a handmaiden to good performance, and since the athletically improving orphan provided an ever-more sizable portion of the latter, he quickly came to enjoy an ever-growing chunk of the former.

In fatherly fashion, Warner endeared himself to Thorpe as mainstream accoutrements powerfully buttressed Thorpe's affection for and loyalty to Warner. Clothes, cuisine, and cash payments neither visible nor available in Indian Territory came in abundance to Thorpe during 1907–1908, convincing him that in the world in which Warner was so adroit, he, too, would be permanently entrenched. Simultaneously, the advantages that Warner heaped upon him helped to deaden the pain and dull the recollection of the deaths that had so darkened Thorpe's first Carlisle years.

Ironically, however, during the 1908–1909 school year, there were cutbacks among those advantages. "Cash flow" problems united with Warner's awareness that sports reformers were not totally blind to his financial chicanery to force him to become temporarily less generous. Thorpe failed to appreciate the reduction in perquisites, especially since he had won Third-Team All-American football honors in 1908 and had captained the 1909 track team, for which he was one of its top two performers. To him, Warner's comparative parsimony was akin to a father's reduction in his child's allowance at the very time the offspring was completing ever-increasing household chores ever-more dutifully.

The prodigal "Pop," as it were, was about to lose a son. Against the wishes of Superintendent Friedman, who had succeeded Mercer in April of 1908 and who had urged a disgruntled Thorpe to remain to complete his program in tailoring, on Sunday, June 13, 1909, he disappeared from Carlisle into the mist of controversy, celebrity, vilification, and, finally, vindication.

SCANDAL AND INFAMY

Baseball, the lone professional sport at the time that adequately paid its performers and the team game Thorpe enjoyed most, could provide a good income while permitting him to do what he loved: compete athletically. Thorpe's two years in Carlisle sports had provided him with the experience and confidence he needed to become the consummate competitor, a professional who could test his skills—and excel—against the world's best while receiving a living wage. Yet, while baseball was to be key in the years immediately ahead, between the first week of September 1911, when Warner lured him back to Carlisle, and December 1912, Thorpe was to emerge as the greatest athlete in the world, a performer whose feats are "the stuff from which dreams are made,"[8] a multi-sport, multi-talented competitor whose equal the world had never seen before. It is not hyperbolic to contend that no other

THE CHERISHED DEAD: JIM THORPE

athlete in the history of sport had or has ever enjoyed greater success over a fifteen-month period.

A second truth surfaced, however, soon thereafter. Warner remained true to form when in January 1913 headlines across the globe proclaimed that Thorpe was no amateur while representing the United States in the 1912 Olympiad. In concert with his longtime friend James Sullivan, a key official in the Amateur Athletic Union (AAU), Warner immediately and successfully acted to protect himself. While totally aware of Thorpe's professional baseball play during the summers of 1909 and 1910, the wily Warner announced that he believed Thorpe had been in Oklahoma during that pair of seasons.

Thorpe—not in 1913, not ever—denied that he had played, first, with Rocky Mount, and, later, with Fayetteville after his departure from Carlisle and before Warner prevailed upon him to return. Equally telling, he had not played under an alias, the strategy most popular among the countless college boys who desired to earn pocket money during summers while teammates or opponents were plying their trade as professional athletes. Nevertheless, in the words of Douglas Noverr, sports historian at Michigan State, Warner "distanced himself" from Thorpe, fearful that, if he did otherwise, he would be ruined as a coach of amateur athletics while inviting equally damaging scrutiny of his financial operations at Carlisle.[9]

Thanks in large measure to Thorpe's accomplishments in football and track and field, Warner was at the height of his game. He was one of the best-paid coaches in the land, and he was not about to sacrifice his future in sports for a twenty-five-year-old Native American who had naively respected and trusted him as a son does a father.

To be sure, Warner could have saved Thorpe from the international scandal that stripped him of his Olympic medals and trophies, but he chose not to, preferring, instead, to save his own skin rather than that of a red-skin. No one could doubt the legally trained, verbally adroit Warner, especially elitists pretending that amateurism existed and could exist in a pure, unadulterated form isolated from financial remuneration; in contrast, countless sports fans raised on stereotypes of Indian cunning and deceit could doubt a questionably educated ward of the United States Government.

Nor did Thorpe's fun-loving, carefree past prove to be an ally, either. His manager at Fayetteville, Charles Clancy, delighted in being central in discussions of Thorpe's alleged professionalism. Cut from the same bigoted cloth as John McGraw, the Baseball Hall of Fame manager for whom Thorpe later played as a New York Giant and who thrived on insults and indignities, Clancy questioned Thorpe's racial purity, proudly proclaiming that "there is a trace of Irish in Thorpe on his paternal side, so he told me." Clancy proceeded in the public press to utter an asininity that only ignorance could spawn: Thorpe "had a yellow streak at times."[10] Like McGraw, Clancy was incapable of fine distinctions, totally unaware, and mentally removed from understanding that Irish blood joined American Indian strains in Thorpe's make-up. Simultaneously, Thorpe's intellectually limited ex-manager had raced to the bizarre conclusion that the Native American exhibited cowardice when he refused to admit he had once played professional baseball at Winston-Salem, North Carolina, a city initially identified with his Eastern Carolina League play but one never represented in that circuit and one the Sac and Fox had never even visited.

There is no evidence that Warner acted to set the record straight for Clancy. Nor did Carlisle's superintendent seem willing to challenge the accuracy of the minor-league manager's sordid description. During the scandal that invited sports fans to question Thorpe's character, Friedman instead proved himself to be Warner's faithful lackey, a far cry from what the honorable Pratt would have been had his Carlisle tenure continued into the first weeks of 1913.

Warner occupied center stage, however, with Sullivan, and the spotlight proved hot as professional baseball was faulted for Thorpe's tragic plight and Warner repetitiously squirmed his way through explanations that he believed Thorpe in Oklahoma, not Carolina, during the summers of 1909 and 1910. The most empathetic contention Warner could announce to the public press was that Thorpe was caught in the throes of what he deemed "a brutal business."[11] Moreover, the most compassionate advice he could provide his confused international icon was that he would be wise to submit a letter of confession to Sullivan and accept the consequences.

Written by Warner, such a letter, carrying Thorpe's signature, was created and, together with a Pontius-Pilate-like letter from Friedman, carried to New York and the AAU potentate. What followed saddened Thorpe but satisfied and saved Warner, Friedman, and Sullivan, and probably elated the vile Clancy: the loss of Thorpe's Olympic awards, his banishment from amateur competition, and elimination of Thorpe's Olympic achievements from all official record books.

Thorpe's expected ignorance—an inexcusable ignorance—was the publicly announced reason for the severe penalties. No explanation, regardless of its accuracy, could negate the fact that the Olympic champion had once taken money for professional baseball play, Sullivan would sanctimoniously proclaim. Thorpe's American Indian bewilderment represented a feeble substitute for the eloquent, but thoroughly hypocritical, pronouncements about the need for and presence of unremunerated amateurism in Olympic competition.

Lurking in the background of the harsh decree were facts never publicized or even acknowledged. The gerrymandered decision was, first and foremost, a concoction of American machinations. With the influential Sullivan and Thorpe's revered coach championing the sanctions, other persons, less potent in amateur athletics, were forced to passivity and hence unquestioning support. The U.S. Olympic Committee endorsed the sanctions; likewise, with reluctance, so did the International Olympic Committee. Sullivan and Warner, with Friedman providing cowardly camaraderie, prevailed, and the IOC, despite voiced objections from outside the United States, added its stamp of approval. Even objective, fair-minded analyses from Sweden, the nation that had hosted the 1912 Olympiad, represented but exercises in futility. Thorpe had sinned, and his punishment was just, according to two of America's unimpeachable authorities: the defender of the nation's amateurism and Thorpe's paternalistic mentor, who grouped the icon with "the boys at the Indian school . . . children mentally."[12]

THORPE'S PLUNGE

Even mental giants, however, had reason to be puzzled. Thorpe, never the fool, recognized without uttering a syllable that Warner had provided him with more cash at Carlisle than he had come close to earning in the financially strapped Eastern Carolina League. Had he been outspoken, and his usual jocular self, he might well have become the first American intercollegiate athlete to proclaim that he took a pay cut when he signed a professional contract! But loyalty and respect—not comedy—dominated his disposition, and he never once publicly challenged Sullivan, Warner, or Friedman and the unfair sanctions the trio of mainstream Americans imposed upon his sports career.

Never made public, either, was a fact no one could contest and no New England blueblood could reject: America's script called for a Caucasian of Anglo ancestry to be the sports hero of the land. Yale's Frank Merriwell, the Burt L. Standish-created athletic phenomenon, broke on the American scene a year before Thorpe's birth but remained firmly implanted in the nation's psyche through 1912, and it was he, fair-skinned and fictional, whom Americans expected and accepted as their ideal rather than an indigenous marvel from Indian Territory. The latter represented an insult to all that was rock solid about the republic that was fast becoming a hope, if not the hope, of the world. Thorpe was by race and color inappropriate to be idolized. Hence, he and similarly minded outsiders best be taught a lesson by the powers of the nation whose Muscular Christianity dictated its destiny.

Related was the embarrassment his school had visited upon the prestige of the universities of the Northeast, many of which would one day emerge as the Ivy League. During 1911, Carlisle had registered football victories over Penn, Harvard, and Brown, and in 1912, Thorpe's 198-point season, a resounding 32–0 trouncing of Brown concluded the campaign. Major universities enrolling and representing the top-tiered baccalaureate-seekers of the nation could not tolerate defeats at the hands of an institution that provided not higher but vocational education, whose students from the far and inconspicuous corners of the continent were hardly the equal of a mediocre junior high school class. Thorpe's censure was simultaneously a tacit communication that the unthinkable and unacceptable would no longer be tolerated by America's premier academic and intellectual bastions.

But the most grievous of errors, the one that sealed Thorpe's fate, was not linked to educational institutions. As an internationally celebrated track and field sensation, Thorpe was irreplaceable to the AAU as it envisioned a team to represent the United States in a worldwide tour after the July Olympiad. No other athlete possessed either his drawing power or his physical prowess, making Thorpe both essential and problematic. Yet, as Bill Thorpe, his son, was to explain often when discussing his father's Olympic scandal, "Dad did what [Warner] requested, and declined, telling stunned AAU officials that he was needed for football at Carlisle."[13] Those officials had vivid recollections of the rejection when reports of Thorpe's professional play emerged less than six months later, and their anger tainted their objectivity. Thorpe deserved punishment, they whispered among themselves, for refusing to comply with their request, and they would see that he received it.

AN IGNOMINIOUS DENOUEMENT

Irony competes with unfairness when that decision gains scrutiny. At Carlisle, Thorpe had unwaveringly preferred baseball to track and field every spring. Warner and he had frequently argued about that preference, with the paternal always triumphing. Baseball offered a future, Thorpe knew. Albert "Chief" Bender, the long-time star hurler for Connie Mack's Philadelphia Athletics and a Carlisle graduate just two years before Thorpe stepped foot on the campus, exemplified a dream-come-true that Thorpe believed he could also enjoy. Yet filial obedience allowed him only a handful of diamond contests during his Carlisle springs.

Headlining the AAU track and field squad, however, Warner would not allow. In effect, he forbade the activities that his ward had never wanted, anyway; in late summer of 1912, when Thorpe was needed in those activities by his country, Warner was adamant. With that refusal Thorpe knew that he was only being moved from one dead-end sport to another: professional football offered no better future than did track and field. Professional football loomed as a huge question mark on the nation's sports horizons, he accurately sensed, and there was feeble indication that it would ever make anyone—player or team owner—anything more than sporadic income. Thorpe, therefore, alienated the AAU officials while obeying Warner. When he did so, he did not realize that his decision would return to sting him so fast and severely.

The severity can easily be appreciated when a late-night incident, occurring months later, rears its tragic head. John Tortes "Chief" Meyers, the Mission, California, Indian, who was Thorpe's New York Giant roommate, volunteered that the usually composed outfielder was "crying . . . with tears . . . rolling down his cheeks" while haltingly uttering: "You know, Chief—the King of Sweden gave me those trophies, he gave them to me. But they took them away from me. They're mine, Chief, I won them fair and square." "It broke his heart," Meyers added, "and he never recovered."[14]

It was not within Thorpe's range of beliefs to acknowledge that in trying to explain why he had done no wrong in 1909 and 1910, he was dealing with men who refused to respect the *fair and square*. The controlling Sullivan, the corrupt Friedman, and the conniving Warner were a self-absorbed trio without appreciation of the morally acceptable. Warner, especially—the mentor to whom Thorpe looked for focus and direction after Hiram P.'s death—was anything but admirable in guiding his ward. It is crucial, also, to emphasize that Warner never expected to set eyes upon Thorpe after Sunday, June 13, 1909, and Thorpe likewise never believed he would fall under Warner's aegis after that date, his five-year Carlisle obligation having ended. But spotted on the streets of Anadarko, Oklahoma, in the late summer of 1911 by his former teammate Albert Exendine, Thorpe was easy prey for his former coach who, on the heels of a 1910 gridiron season that saw Carlisle claim only eight wins in fourteen tries, knew his football hopes could quickly brighten with the return of the performer who had grown so much physically that he was labeled as "big as a mule."[15] Warner wanted Thorpe back at Carlisle not for what he could do for the twenty-four-year-old but for what the twenty-four-year-old could do to save his job—and just maybe bring him additional glory as the coach of an Olympic star. Thorpe did not disappoint him; he disappointed Thorpe.

UPON REFLECTION

Indeed, Warner's image remains untarnished, even to this day. Countering, dodging, and deflecting the dozens of questions hurled his way as Carlisle came under ever-closer scrutiny as a result of Thorpe's scandal—a scrutiny that finally led to the closing of the institution in 1919—Warner razzle-dazzled his way through an embarrassing four-win 1914 football season, only to announce immediately thereafter that he could not resist an offer from the University of Pittsburgh to coach its gridiron team. Leaving Carlisle with a record of seventy-eight victories in one hundred contests (and a record of forty-three wins, just five losses, and two ties during Thorpe's four-year varsity career), Warner continued to project an image that belied the truth: a manipulator of young men who, while refining their athletic skills because of his genius, satisfied a narcissistic mania: "Notwithstanding his occasional illusions of omnipotence, the narcissist depends on others to validate his self-esteem. He cannot live without an admiring audience. His apparent freedom from family ties and institutional constraints does not free him to stand alone or glory in his individuality. On the contrary, it contributes to his insecurity, which he can overcome only by seeing his grandiose self reflected in the attention of others, or by attaching himself to those who radiate celebrity, power, and charisma. For the narcissist, the world is a mirror."[16]

For Warner, the athletic *boys* of Carlisle, especially Thorpe, offered a reflection of his (not their) prowess, and it was the carefree, competitive, charismatic Sac and

Fox—the incomparable star—to whom he most closely attached himself and in whose glory he bathed most glowingly. Because of the disclosures of professionalism, it was not within his moral capabilities either to defend him or, later, to call him the best football player he ever coached—Ernie Nevers of Stanford earned that distinction—but it was with and through the loyal Thorpe that he enjoyed his most prized successes and his most ego-escalating achievements. Warner fathered Thorpe, and Thorpe, in turn, made his "Pop" proud and famous.

Yet neither the honorable athlete nor his unscrupulous mentor today, less than a decade into the third millennium, enjoys the celebrity that has been visited upon today's multisport stars. Admittedly, "Pop Warner Football," a creation the wily coach introduced in 1929, well into his coaching career, continues to keep his name before America's undeveloped footballers and their parents, but, because of its focus on youth, it understandably fails to capture the headlines and hype enjoyed by its more skillful adult counterparts—the multibillion-dollar enterprises known as intercollegiate and NFL football. Nonetheless, through the coast-to-coast leagues, the nation continues to mouth the name of Carlisle's most famous mentor and, invariably, to learn about his coaching feats and his supposed genius at molding citizens, especially Native Americans, of which the Republic can be proud.

Yet his most famous prodigy and product, Thorpe, retains a far more unusual place, a unique one, in the human psyche. Although he had been dead for over half-a-century, humans on virtually every continent refuse to forget that combination of bizarre happenings embracing vilification and, thirty long years after his passing, vindication: his brain-boggling excellence in so many athletic endeavors and at so many levels—amateur, intercollegiate, professional, and global—culminating in the injustice with which he was forced to live the last four decades of his life, a disgrace brought to a fortunate end only after the power structure of amateur athletics of the world decades later concluded he had been wronged by its predecessors. Like no other athlete ever, he fires the imagination while tugging at the conscience; every youth, particularly every youth in the nation he represented in the 1912 Olympiad, yearns to be his athletic equal, yet simultaneously cringes at the thought of being dogged by unjust scandal during the bulk of his or her adulthood.

The contrast featuring the ultimate in success and the despicable in consequences brings both a joy and a sorrow not comfortably accommodated in the human mind. Thorpe's bittersweet saga possesses a power that periodically forces it to the surface for public scrutiny, a timelessness so firmly entrenched in the annals of sport that it appears incapable of disappearing. Today's Thorpe-like athletic celebrities, however, are creations and beneficiaries of media outlets not yet imagined by inventors during the age of Muscular Christianity. Television, particularly, has magnified the prowess and personality of athletes who literally merit, in Andy Warhol's famous phrase, just fifteen minutes of fame but, instead, gain season upon season of it, performers who no more play for the love of sport but, rather for the fame, finance, and security it affords them.

The aforementioned Bo Jackson and Deion Sanders, merely two examples of this trend, though certainly talented and groundbreaking in their own right, have received the majority of the attention, if not the munificence, of all that the late twentieth century and the early years of the twenty-first can bestow upon athletes of talent who parlay prowess and publicity into immortality. Jim Thorpe was born eight decades too soon to benefit from these clearly modern rewards, monetary and otherwise, to which they have had access. His error thus lies not in signing a professional contract in 1909 but, rather, in being born into an era less just, less technologically advanced, and—most important of all—more convinced that the athlete could and should play for the pure love of sport. Merriwell—and his fictionalized values—reigned, a domination the new millennium refuses to acknowledge.

Three decades after his death, Thorpe's family received the recast Olympic awards he had won in 1912 and his name was returned to Olympic records, the lone Olympian ever to triumph in both the decathlon and the pentathlon. With those actions of the 1980s, as Jackson and Sanders were romping to both multisport and multimillion-dollar success, the most accomplished of all multisport performers again raced into the minds of the world's sports fans—vindicated at long last, free of blemish for the first time in seventy years and thus again worthy of the awe and superlatives that he had inspired during the two decades he had been the athletic marvel of the globe.

Fan attention, however, quickly returned to Bo, Deion, and the other performers who, off the field as well as on it, could be paraded in the flesh across the countless screens to which today's "couch potatoes" and "bar flies" are addicted, heroes and antiheroes invariably as blustery as they are ego-inflated. In the five-minute memory, Thorpe returned to the distant past, a once-had-been whose achievements lay hidden at the bottom of the recent and immediate whom television reruns could keep before the public's eye and in its cranium. Ironically, however, the years have brought him a respect and admiration rarely afforded the palpably cleanest modern performer.

Even the mania for contemporary heroes and histrionics cannot obliterate either the injustice with which Thorpe lived during the bulk of his life or his domination of a sports world dimly recalled in the new millennium. Always for the relative few with a passion for justice and objectivity, he will remain "a physical mutation,"[17] as biographer Robert L. Whitman once termed him, "The Greatest Athlete in the World,"[18] as Sweden's King Gustav originally labeled him, and, most accurate of all, "the greatest all-around athlete in the history of sports, dating back to Coroebus of Elis in the eighth century before the birth of Christ,"[19] the description sports historian Murray Olderman offered a few years back.

Regardless of how aggressively or creatively they are hyped, it is increasingly unlikely that either Jackson or Sanders or any other modern athlete will ever merit those lustrous epithets, if only for the stench that celebrity tends to foist upon the famously overexposed. Expediency indeed invites the cliché, and while time may tell, time may not be afforded that luxury, either. Thorpe excelled in an era markedly different from that one in which Jackson and Sanders performed, so different that comparisons can be but speculative. In 1912, when he gained the label with which he was forever to be identified, "The greatest athlete in the world," and even in 1920, when at age thirty-three, he reluctantly agreed to serve as the first president of what was to burgeon into the National Football League, there were but two media through which Thorpe's athletic feats could be reliably communicated: print and telegraph. Unless one were an eyewitness to his performances or learned about them through word of mouth, the world's publics—for their sports reporting and editorializing—depended upon what in the new millennium are laughably primitive modes of communication. In its infancy was film, so unsophisticated that virtually no fan today believes it worth his or her time to view the countless "still shots" taken of Thorpe or the grainy, blurred silent footage depicting him receiving his Olympic awards from Sweden's monarch; and even in 1929, when he formally retired from professional competition, that medium was but a shadow of what it has become in the "You Tube" age.

Immeasurably different, also, are the managers of professional teams. Gone, never to be tolerated again, are the martinets like Clancy, his minor-league manager, and John McGraw, the New York Giant manager for whom Thorpe played (or, rather, sat on the bench) during his first years in the Major Leagues. Such leaders were the norm at the turn of the twentieth century, demeaning, demanding dictators whose word no player dared to defy. Their iron hand and rule even permitted them access to players' personal mail, an experience to which Thorpe fell victim, and it routinely allowed them to curse and malign their charges eyeball to eyeball, as well as to police them in their free hours, two additional occurrences that Thorpe experienced but refused to tolerate.

More important, agents and endorsements, fixtures of our modern age, were unknown until technology brought athletic competition into living rooms, dens, and bars. Television, especially, has transformed humans, whose parents and grandparents possessed little knowledge of and less interest in sports at any level, into enthusiasts anxious to spend limitless hours and dollars on any endeavor resembling an athletic competition, including poker, hot-dog eating contests, fixed and fraudulent wrestling matches, or the "anything-goes, no-holds-barred, wild-man" ring confrontations that are the Ultimate Fighting circuits. Multimillion-dollar contracts and multiyear commitments have emerged as the norm, not the exception, and Jackson, Sanders, and countless other competitors have been the beneficiaries. As such, too, they enjoy freedoms unknown in Thorpe's era, in which no professional athlete was ever "allowed to do just about anything he wanted,"[20] although the pratfalls appear to begin with the daily twenty-four-hour news cycle whose guarantee is that few can live up to the expectations behind the dollars, either.

Bo, Deion, and their counterparts, however, are not to be faulted. Technology has united with marketing to drown the nation and the rest of the civilized world in what they now crave: submersion in the waters of athletics, minor or major. But those waters are transparent. John and Jane Q. Public can see as well as hear what in Thorpe's era only sportswriter Grantland Rice and golden-voiced Bill Stern, like their lesser-known media predecessors and contemporaries, could discern and decipher. Yet, not content with almost total access to what occurs on the athletic field, they also make claims on the personal and the confidential, demanding not only to violate and perceive privacy but also to impose standards and judgments. Stereotyping is inevitable. Norms and—more problematic, even—the expectations of the John and Jane Q's have evolved, and deviations are no longer to be tolerated. Vulnerable particularly because of the monies that they accrue, contemporary athletes are easy targets for middle-class fans raised amidst the nostalgia of the athlete-as-Merriwell paradigm who also elect to study and idolize them, if only to soon learn that these disposable heroes are, in fact, human beings, with feet of clay, muscles with moles, and toes without twinkles.

Athletes of color like Jackson and Sanders, America and much of the civilized world tacitly proclaim, must be especially spotless in their behaviors. Outside the stadiums in which "the roar of the crowd" celebrates their achievements, they realize that racial bias can suddenly and inexplicably surface if they but challenge what mainstream citizens expect or respect. Individuality can be a detriment to adulation, can be a "Yes, but" conversation-turnabout should they not be impeccable in habit, dress, or discourse.

Thorpe refused to be anything other than what his tribal upbringing had taught him to be: simple and concise of speech; generous even when disadvantaged; humble and honest regardless of audience; loyal and silent even in the face of adversity; fun-loving in the company of friends and family; and aggressive and combative when derided, mocked, demeaned, or challenged. Gentleness, not meanness, characterized his make-up. He made few demands on people; simplicity was his norm, his "comfort zone," to borrow from the contemporary vernacular.

That he was abandoned and vilified by people with different values—Caucasians more worldly, cosmopolitan, and "realistic"—should be viewed as tragic, a misfortune that his disposition, race, and era made virtually inevitable; nonetheless, it also merits the label "patently unfair." What was visited upon Thorpe was and remains indefensible. In a morally enriched environment, he may have fared differently. Too, in more objective settings, it is inconceivable that today's once and future phenoms could not retain some semblance of what they value most and what the powers and public seldom allowed Thorpe to enjoy in his era: distinctiveness.

In 2007, Kenneth Shropshire declares in the subtitle of his *Being Sugar Ray* that the talented Robinson, definitely a distinctive figure outside as well as inside the boxing ring, was *The First Celebrity Athlete*, a contention difficult to accept when Thorpe's worldwide acclaim was once so unique that even Vatican dignitaries yearned to see and visit with him on his 1913–1914 baseball tour across the globe with McGraw's Giants. Yet it is also easy to agree with Shropshire when he maintains that "Celebrity is complex, but it is also about being who you are, you being something people—not just white people—like."[21] Everyone but the ruling Caucasian elite enjoyed Thorpe, his affability, accessibility, and humility representing welcome, refreshing accompaniments to the headline-making athletic achievements that, in a haughtier human, would have mandated isolation from the masses. Everyone, too, likes today's stars, if not for the same reasons, for ones a time period different from Thorpe's accepts and supports, monetarily and otherwise. In the case of Bo Jackson, irrespective of race, he grew to become, in an almost folkloric sense, the most knowledgeable mortal ever conceived, thanks to a marketing coup that made him millions and Nike, AT&T, and Pepsi-Cola even more. As he was to indicate in his 1991 biography *Bo Knows Bo*, co-written by the late Dick Schaap, "Bo certainly knows business."[22]

But so does Sanders. Yet objections to his on-the-field antics have not kept him from the spotlight, the acclaim, and the equally flashy sums he has earned for a distinctiveness previously reserved for offensive brilliance rather than for his uniquely defensive *joie de vivre*.

In this new millennium, as athletic prowess continues to be measured through the ever-evolving eye of modern technology and its mercurial relationship with celebrity, no such advantage comes to Thorpe, save for the march of time, which may yet prove to be the greatest ally his legacy ever enjoyed. Indeed, that the death of his 101-year-old second wife, Freeda Kirkpatrick Thorpe (on March 3, 2007), was reported by mainstream media, sometimes with pictures of the woman whom Thorpe had met and married when she was but a teenager, speaks volumes about how the Thorpe figure has reemerged to continue to fascinate the contemporary imagination. Similarly, the definitive biography of Thorpe promised by the meticulous Kate Buford, author of a comparable volume on Hollywood star Burt Lancaster, and the documentary on Thorpe for which Joe Bruchac, the versatile Native American writer and publisher, is currently preparing the script, both provide convincing evidence that yesteryear's phenomenon will merit public perusal far into the future, probably for as long as sport itself survives. Thus, while in the decades to come, digitally enhanced video footage will undoubtedly bestow a visibility and vitality upon modern and contemporary athletic superstars, these decidedly more graphic and convincing depictions are not necessarily destined to be more poignant, more powerful, or more memorable than the fleeting glimpses of a since-rehabilitated Jim Thorpe, who has, ironically, come to stand as the epitome of the American athletic tradition.

NOTES

1. Bo Jackson and Dick Schaap, *Bo Knows Bo* (New York: Jove Books, 1991), 173.

2. Dave Kindred, "50 Years Go Fast When You're Watching Baseball," *Sporting News*, 12 April 2004.

3. Alaine Goodale Eastman, *Pratt, The Red Man's Moses* (Norman: University of Oklahoma Press, 1935).

4. David Wallace Adams, *Education for Extinction: American Indians and the Boarding School Experience, 1875–1928* (Lawrence: University of Kansas Press, 1995), 323–24.

5. "Outings" are discussed in numerous authoritative sources. Probably the most detailed description appears in Genevieve Bell's "Telling Stories Out of School: Remembering the Carlisle Indian Industrial School, 1879–1918." Ph.D. diss. Stanford University, 1998. More concise, but equally accurate, descriptions appear in a number of sources, including Joseph B. Oxendine, *American Indian Sports Heritage* (Champaign: Human Kinetics Books, 1988), 208–9; Robert W. Reising, *Jim Thorpe: Tar Heel* (Rocky Mount: Communique, Inc., 1974), 28–29; Jack Newcombe, *The Best of the Athletic Boys* (Garden City, NY: Doubleday, 1975), 71–73; and Sally Jenkins, *The Real All Americans* (New York: Doubleday, 2007), 100.

6. Bill Crawford, *All American: The Rise and Fall of Jim Thorpe* (Hoboken: Wiley, 2005), 61.

7. Quoted in Robert W. Wheeler, *Jim Thorpe, World's Greatest Athlete* (Norman: University of Oklahoma Press, 1975). 41.

8. William Shakespeare, "The Tempest," IV, I (written in 1610 and/or 1611). Hollywood star Humphrey Bogart popularized the phrase for modern and contemporary audiences in *The Maltese Falcon*, the Warner Brothers movie of 1941.

9. Douglas Noverr, conversation with author, East Lansing, MI, November 14, 2003.

10. Crawford, *All American*, 198–200.

11. Jenkins, *The Real All Americans*, 288.

12. Crawford, *All American*, 205.

13. Bill Thorpe, conversation with author, Stroud, Oklahoma, April 23, 2000.

14. Wheeler, *Thorpe*, 158.

15. Wheeler, *Thorpe*, 80.

16. Christopher Lasch, *The Culture of Narcissism* (New York: W. W. Norton and Company, Inc., 1978), 10.

17. Quoted in a televised round-table discussion with Jack Thorpe and the author at the University of North Carolina at Pembroke, March 28, 1953.

18. Quoted in a variety of sources, including Robert L. Whitman's *Jim Thorpe: Athlete of the Century* (Defiance, Ohio: Robert L. Whitman in cooperation with the Jim Thorpe Association, 2002), 53.

19. No author, "Biography of Jim Thorpe," http://www.jimthorpeassopc.org/JimThorpe/index .html (July 25, 2007).

20. Jackson and Schaap, *Bo Knows*, 231.

21. Kenneth Shropshire, *Being Sugar Ray: The Life of Sugar Ray Robinson, America's Greatest Boxer and the First Celebrity Athlete* (New York: Basic Civitas Books, 2007), 219.

22. Jackson and Schaap, *Bo Knows*, 174.

PART III

THE LIVING MODELS

BILL RUSSELL

From Revulsion to Resurrection

MURRY NELSON

INTRODUCTION

In the 1960s, Bill Russell was considered by most to be the most dominant player
in basketball. His Boston Celtics were the undisputed champions of the sport and
exemplified the competitive zeal so storied in American lore. Yet Russell was largely
disliked by many fans and often excoriated in the media. His seemingly somber
demeanor, his outspokenness, particularly on issues of race and racial equality, and
his intimidating presence won him very few friends, though he quickly won the
respect of his peers.

Russell proved to be an active supporter of the civil rights movement, which
aroused some people negatively. In addition, there were those who claimed that a
large influx of African Americans would "ruin" the beauty of basketball. This was
simply code for racism, especially given that the Celtics were more typically noted
for playing the ultimate in team basketball with Russell generally being the one
regarded as the team leader. Nevertheless, their winning ways also raised feelings
of jealousy and near hatred among fans of the other seven NBA teams. Russell,
a reluctant foil, remained a lightning rod of controversy, most of it negative and
fervently racially based.

Twenty years later, however, Russell's perceived public persona was viewed
much more positively. He became a grand veteran of the professional basketball
wars, an extremely successful player who was not able to match that same success
as either a coach or a general manager. He was basketball's biggest winner who was
subjected to the same caprice as anyone else might have been. No longer viewed as
aloof, however, he came to be viewed as practically approachable and even revered,
an insightful icon of the professional game and an impressionable culture. He certainly had the respect of everyone associated with the game of basketball as well as
many fans of the sport in general, but how can we account for such change? Was
it that Russell himself was changing, or was it perhaps part and parcel of a more

widespread cultural shift? Moreover, and more on point, how was it possible that the world of sports and media could converge to construct a decidedly different view of Bill Russell than the guy Americans had once known? The answers to these complex queries lie somewhere between these realms and require a much more thorough examination.

BACKGROUND

William Felton Russell was born in 1934 outside Monroe, Louisiana, where the entire family, and most specifically the men, experienced firsthand the sort of everyday acts of discrimination and potential violence that came to mark Jim Crow Louisiana. By 1943 his family would move out of the South and into the East Bay area of Oakland, California, as part of the Great Migration out of the South that many African Americans undertook in search of steady employment. Despite leaving the South so early in his life, young Bill remained acutely aware of the sort of discrimination practiced there on an overt basis and soon discovered analogous discrimination practiced more covertly outside the region.

At an early age Russell, who was raised along with his brother by their father following their mother's untimely death, was captivated by athletics, but he was a gawky, awkward young teen who grew faster than his coordination could handle. He failed to excel at football, baseball, or even cheerleading, all endeavors he would try at one time or another, but, through the kindness of a junior high basketball coach, he landed the last spot on the team in his sophomore year. From there, he would advance all the way to the varsity of what would become a most storied McClymonds High School sporting tradition.

Despite being 6′6″ upon graduation and a part-time starter, there was no interest on the part of any colleges for him to play basketball upon his graduation. This was still an age in which fewer than 5 percent of African American high school graduates would go on to become college graduates,[1] and the lack of interest in Russell was disheartening to both Russell and his father since they had promised their late wife/mother that he would attend college and be the first college graduate in either side of the family. Nevertheless, without offers, Russell went to work in the steel mills alongside his father with no hope for a more prosperous future.

Unexpectedly, a University of San Francisco representative, who had witnessed Russell's best high school performance, arranged for a tryout for Russell with head basketball coach Phil Woolpert. Though Russell did not perform all that well, Woolpert and freshmen coach Ross Gaudice saw potential in the now 6′9″ young man who was if nothing else a most determined worker. He was offered and accepted a scholarship to USF beginning in the fall of 1952, though at the time it had fewer than twenty-five African American students in a total population of just under 3,000.[2]

At that time, almost all African Americans enrolled in American colleges attended historically black colleges and universities (HBCUs), so in this regard Russell, who was one of two black players on the team, was a trendsetter from early on. He was fortunate that the West Coast seemed to be more benign in its racist practices than other areas of the country as students and alumni of USF were generally tolerant, if not outright ambivalent, of his presence on campus. Still, Russell was generally quiet and introverted in large part because he did not wish to draw attention to himself, no easy task considering his height and color in that particular milieu.

Russell's roommate, and subsequent best friend, was K. C. Jones, another African American with whom Russell would play through his entire college and professional career. Together they faced a string of slights—overt or otherwise—as would be expected in a 1950s-era California career. By most accounts, however, though they were cast in this often untenable situation, it would be not the racial connotations but rather the basketball ramifications of their presence at USF and hence the Celtics that would help alter the course of first the college and later the professional game.

K. C. Jones missed most of their first season together, Russell's sophomore season, following an emergency appendectomy while Russell's other teammates on the varsity, perhaps concerned for their own basketball futures, did little to encourage the nascent skills for which Russell would later be known. And in spite of the fact that they were a veteran team with a new center who had set several freshmen scoring records the year prior, they ended up finishing a disappointing 14 and 7.

By the next year, however, Jones returned, the players who had disrupted the team chemistry had graduated, and Russell was blossoming into a better and smarter player. The team went 28 and 1, losing only to UCLA early in the season and closing with 26 consecutive victories and the NCAA championship. Only at this point did Russell begin to get national recognition as a basketball player.

Media coverage was much less predominant in 1955, especially in the East since many scores came in after Eastern fans and newspapers were already put to bed. What coverage there was usually focused on the Pacific Coast Conference (now the Pac-10), so USF and Russell were, in the parlance of sport, flying under the radar for the most part until the finals of the NCAA Tournament. But as USF continued to amass victories, it became harder to ignore the changes taking place in the Bay Area.[3]

Many of the biggest college conferences were still segregated, and those that were integrated had very few African Americans on their teams. The Pacific Coast Conference, for example, had a smattering of blacks with one or two on most of their squads. At that time USF played in the West Coast Athletic Conference, which was composed of smaller universities, a number of which had some religious affiliation. African Americans seemed to be tolerated, if not necessarily embraced, by universities such as Santa Clara, St. Mary's and Russell's own Jesuit-governed USF. In contrast, while the Big Ten had integrated within the past ten years, the

Southeastern, Atlantic Coast, and Southwestern Conferences were still segregated, and some schools simply would not play against teams with blacks and, thus,
would not play in the NCAA Tournament as black players continued to distin-
guish themselves.

CELEBRITY

After sweeping through the conference undefeated in 1954, the Dons then won
five games in the NCAA tournament to become national champions, defeating
defending champion LaSalle in the finals in Kansas City. Russell was voted MVP
of the tournament as well as First Team All-American. Suddenly he was becoming
a national figure in college basketball while the run-up to the next season would
focus much more on him, which in retrospect must have offered some divergent
and certainly confusing moments for the young man. For example, during the summer he was invited to the White House to represent college basketball as President
Eisenhower recognized athletes from all sports at a luncheon. Following that, the
entire Russell family, including his stepmother and his future wife Rose, drove back
to the Bay Area from Washington via Louisiana to visit relatives. Russell found that,
despite his growing celebrity and having just won a national championship and
being named to the All-American team, he was still just a black man and discriminated against openly. This angered and embittered him, and he began to notice
more acutely the effects of discrimination throughout his college career.[4]

Early in the 1956 season *Time* magazine published an article about Russell that
for the most part introduced the nation to the burgeoning star. Throughout, Russell was presented as a poor Negro boy who had little possibility for greatness in
basketball because of being subjected to the segregation of the South, a most fa-
vored technique among more liberalized writers of the day. By moving to Oakland, it was noted, his prospects were greatly enhanced, but in presenting such a
tone, *Time* both reinforced stereotypes and allayed fears that many whites had of
blacks by referring to Russell as a "happy-go-lucky string bean."[5] The article also—
correctly—portrayed Russell as introverted and self-deprecating off the court which
seemed to soften his growing on-court reputation as a fierce shot blocker and tough
competitor.

Time would go on to publish yet another piece on Russell following the university's second consecutive national championship in 1956, but this piece had a
decidedly different air to it. In it Russell was referred to as "lazily turning in a
26 point performance," implying in the most racialized sense that it was Russell's
natural talent that made him as good as he was and not the hours of work that he
had put into improving his game since his junior high years.[6] Indeed, the images
being constructed of Russell were showing him to be a benign behemoth, but while
they could be somewhat flattering in their praise of his athletic talent, they were also

tempered with a subtle racism. And when he spoke to the media or was represented by them, most of the talk was on his basketball background with some details of his early life thrown in to emphasize his blackness first while everything else stood idly around the periphery of his story.

In 1956 Russell deferred his entrance to the professional ranks in order to play on the U.S. Olympic basketball team in Melbourne, Australia, where he helped the U.S. win a gold medal. The Olympics were not given a lot of media coverage, given that they were on the other side of the world. In addition the U.S. had won every basketball game in Olympic competition since the advent of the sport in the games in 1936. Thus, Russell's contributions to the team, while appreciated on a sporting level, were, nonetheless, underappreciated in most other circles. Still, he returned to the States in December 1956 determined to get his career underway, and through a sequence of events, some of which were steeped in racialized happenstance, he would soon join the Boston Celtics.

By the time he joined the Celtics, there were only seven African Americans in the league (a scant 7 percent), with three on the New York roster alone.[7] In this respect, his being African American worked for both the Celtics and Russell. Boston, stratified as it would prove to be, was still a better place for him to work than the team that originally drafted him, the then St. Louis Hawks. St. Louis remained the southernmost city in the NBA and continued to practice the time-honored traditions of Jim Crow, and while the NBA draft in those days was typically a regional one, the Celtics were able to lure him away from the Hawks by in a sense using the racial climate as a valuable chip, a move that would ultimately set the stage for both Russell's and the team's future in what was then conceived of as a more tolerant city for an African American to work in spite of the reality.

Irrespective of all the maneuvering, Boston would prove to be equally as challenging a place for Russell and his family to establish their roots. Russell was the first African American on the Celtics and initially had to live in a hotel, though he would eventually move his family out to Reading, a modest yet nonetheless suburban area of Boston, where they were more tolerated than welcomed. While Boston's fans appreciated the basketball efforts, Russell's inability or unwillingness to warm to them offered the allusion that he was aloof while fitting the then-popular stereotype of the "uppity black man" who didn't seem to know his place. Moreover, he found similar difficulties outside of Boston as more and more fans of the NBA worked from the then-popular assumption that black styles of ball playing would alter the constructed aesthetic of beauty and teamwork of the game, again terms that come loaded with racial assumptions, though in hindsight Russell had already proven to be in effect the embodiment of the more traditional and conservative values that many felt were being threatened by an encroaching black presence in the sport.

Russell was certainly not the first or only African American measured against this arbitrary standard. University of Cincinnati All-American and subsequent NBA Hall-of-Famer Oscar Robertson too talked about the quota system that was being

MURRY NELSON

implemented for black players at the various colleges who had recruited him.[8] Fitz-patrick discusses these same stereotypes in reference to Texas Western and their all black starting five in 1966.[9] Still, this stereotyping hardly describes Bill Russell and his teammate at both USF and later the Celtics, K. C. Jones. The two had philoso-phized, analyzed, and theorized about basketball since they had roomed together in college, and they saw the game as a game of angles and advantages, the way future coaches would. Nevertheless, to basketball fans who had grown accustomed to a segregated game in most collegiate circuits and in the professional game, there re-mained a white, more proper, game in spite of the fact that what Russell and Jones were helping to foment was exactly that. Still, for most observers and fans alike, the supposed capriciousness of the so-called Negro game was unseemly, and it would take a number of years for Russell to overcome this misconception in spite of the incredible successes he would experience as a Celtic.

In Russell's thirteen years as a player, including his last three years as player-coach, (something that would too have significant racial connotations), Russell's Celtics won eleven NBA championships, a record unprecedented in any profes-sional sports history. Over time, fans begrudgingly admitted that the Celtics played great *team* basketball and that Russell, with his dominant defense and tenacious competitiveness, was the linchpin of those teams. Thus, the Celtics and he, like so many other players and franchises that have become synonymous with dominance, i.e. baseball's Yankees, hockey's Canadians, football's Cowboys, began to engender dislike or hatred because of that very same degree of success. As a result, Russell came to be viewed in a most negative light due in no small part to the jealousy of some while facing the assumption that continued to suggest that a black man could not and should not be seen as the embodiment of excellence regardless of the cir-cumstances. But, as it became more and more evident that African Americans could play basketball in the way the so-called purists continued to envision, the criticisms of Russell in this vein grew much more muted and soon disappeared.

CONSTRUCTING A DEMON

Off the court, what seems to have haunted Russell more than anything else during his playing days was his candor when it came to justice and civil rights. His com-mitment to the civil rights movement alienated many in middle America and led some to perceive him as just another radical Negro using his very public perch to criticize American life. But while there were those who saw civil liberties only in the abstract, Russell had seen racial discrimination firsthand, and he was resolute in his support for change.

Though for the most part Russell remained unaligned, the movement did not really gain the kind of attention and support it needed until the early 1960s. At that time the more radical of two civil rights factions was identified with Malcolm

92

X and the Black Muslims, from whom Malcolm later split. The other, more traditional faction was identified with Martin Luther King, Jr., and his positions on nonviolence.

At a time when black Americans came to support either the more aggressive black power movement as exemplified in the efforts of Malcolm X and the Muslims or the more spiritual-based nonviolent practices as expressed through the efforts of Dr. King and his followers, Russell found himself perched in the middle of such challenges. Unwilling to choose sides, Russell spoke supportively of both Malcolm X and Dr. King, which was rare for this period. Still, he often showed flashes of a sort of militancy that belied his support for Dr. King and his membership in organizations such as the NAACP, landing him in terms of the public eye more toward the side of the more militant factions. Still, and in what would become more the norm for him, Russell affirmed that he was not a leader in civil rights but viewed the movement as single in aim regardless of the appearance of various factions and subgroups. For him, the positions expressed by all sides of the movement were not divisive but rather represented a search for the most effective way to achieve the aim of equal opportunity, something that garnered him both approval and scorn from an increasingly more anxious public.[10]

To the shock of many white Americans Russell in a 1963 article published in *Sports Illustrated* admitted that in many ways he was probably more closely aligned with the more militant wings of the struggle than many had hoped. As he would tell *SI* writer Gilbert Rogin, "[A] lot of the things that [the Black Muslims] say express the way that I feel perfectly."[11] Still, he was hardly one to take a hard line. For example, he disagreed with the Muslim position that the white man is a devil, but he did admit that given his circumstances that he disliked most white people while showing a fondness for most black people through the mechanism of solidarity. That he would admit this is in the widely circulated pages of a popular sport magazine did little in terms of his desire to reach out to more white Americans.

Russell's opposition to the war in Vietnam proved to be yet another source of public disdain. He spoke openly and wrote industriously while explaining his position on the war and, in parallel, his support for Muhammad Ali and his struggle to gain conscientious objector status. For a middle America raised on the cultural myths that placed piety and patriotism as a large part of the athletic mystique, this was unconscionable. Still, it was very much in keeping with Russell's established pattern of outspokenness and willingness to involve himself outside the athletic domain. In an age of new Negroes and new challenges to the status quo, Russell the athlete had come to exemplify both excellence on the field and a conscience off it regardless of the cost.

That Russell openly encouraged others to keep pushing for equality first while continuing the struggle in spite of small gains further alienated an increasingly angst-ridden populace. For many, when Russell spoke of justice, they would define it as justice for minorities while leaving white America to foot the bill, a most unpopular position indeed. He excoriated the NBA, claiming, probably accurately, that there were quotas on the number of Negroes acceptable to the league on each team's roster as well as on the floor at any one time. In this respect, Russell could further be portrayed as surly yet at the same time could also be shown to be self-righteous enough that he could easily push others aside rather than seem grateful for what he had.

Indeed, Russell was seen by some white observers to epitomize the ungrateful Negro ballplayer, and they felt even more distant and distrustful of him in spite of the fact that it was their white privilege that afforded them the perch from which to view Russell in such a manner. In the eyes of some, this notably outspoken athlete, in an age still governed by a policy of benign acquiescence on the part of most nonwhite performers, was equally as guilty of racism, a charge that certainly (and somewhat ironically) did not fit many people's image of the conventional sports hero. The view may have been archaic, but Russell seemed to be shattering it with every comment.

To be sure, the way Russell was being represented in the American press did little to help soften his image, and this was true across the political divide. For example, in a 1965 piece in the *Nation*, a publication known for left-leaning polemics, there was a description of Russell as the owner of a 1,500-acre rubber plantation in Liberia. The piece entitled "Ol' Massa Russell" ended sardonically by speculating that upon his retirement, he would "sip mint juleps on the front porch of his Liberian mansion as he listens to the field hands singing after it is too dark to work."[12] Ironically, the ramifications of such a critique could be brought home fairly easily. His second trip through the Deep South in 1962, for instance, a virtual replica of the one he took in his college days, vividly demonstrated to him the dichotomy of his being successful and black in America. He lamented the whole way that he and his sons could not find places to eat or to sleep even though he continued to be recognized wherever he stopped.

By this stage of his career, many writers seemed much more interested in tearing down his image rather than in presenting the genuine Bill Russell to their readership. In the aforementioned *Sports Illustrated* article, for instance, Rogin, despite offering a generally positive view of Russell, nevertheless, felt it important to emphasize that Russell "lives on a white block in a white town, has white baby-sitters [sic] and drives a 1964 Lincoln Continental convertible."[13] While on the one hand indicating that Russell was a success in spite of the obstacles before him, the continued presence of a racial undergirding remained problematic and helped foster, or at least maintain, the image that Russell was the type of man that the pubic generally was not going to get close to let alone understand. This in turn served to reinforce the notion that irrespective of his success on the court, he would be afforded very little success off it.

To be sure, Russell was extremely proud of his accomplishments and went to great lengths to both demonstrate and justify such pride. He was fond of telling others that he was in many respects a self-made man, hardly the picture of the traditional Negro male to which Americans had grown accustomed. Time and again he would respond to his critics, exclaiming that ability not entitlements put him in the public eye while also filling a much-needed role as a spokesperson for the so-deemed new Negro athlete. As he would exclaim in the aptly entitled "I Owe the Public Nothing," "The first thing we (as Negroes in sport) have to get rid of . . . is the idea that this is a popularity contest. I don't work for acceptance. It doesn't make any difference whether the fans like me or not."[14]

A POST-CAREER RUSSELL

The iconic Russell cast in the public space would change, albeit subtly, in 1966 when he was named player-coach of the Celtics. That a black man could lead a ballclub without playing was still far on the horizon in those earlier years. Still, that Russell could be tapped for such a position was in and of itself noteworthy. Nevertheless, as coach, he was required to make more media appearances, though in many respects the most basic aspects of his character went unaltered. He remained outspoken, did not give autographs, as was his policy established early in his career (which many found extremely imprudent), and continued to exhibit a mix of introversion and guardedness around strangers.

That year he would also publish the first of his two autobiographies in which he would more elegantly make his case regarding racism in the United States while asserting with equal clarity his case for why it was that the Celtics, more than any other franchise in professional basketball, were exemplary, something that made him even more unpopular with those already suspicious of his behavior and his motives. It should be noted too, however, that this same outspokenness gained him the admiration of those who had, ironically enough, grown to appreciate his team-oriented style of play and others who were simply tired of athletes whose memoirs were either tell-alls or filled with banal and nostalgic fluff.

In 1969, after having won yet another NBA championship and after three years of serving as player-coach of the most storied franchise in NBA history, Russell retired. Unlike the more modern era in which the elder statesmen of various games are afforded a sort of farewell tour upon announcing their retirement, Russell wanted no such hue and cry claiming that it would have inevitably detracted from both his notion of team first while distracting him (and perhaps even the team) from the job at hand.[15]

Soon after retirement, Russell left the Boston area, where he never felt at home despite his successes, and moved back to California—Southern California—where he engaged in various entertainment industry jobs including some film and television appearances and a talk radio show, which he hosted on the Los Angeles airwaves. Talk radio seemed almost too perfect for Russell as it offered him a chance to express his views while engaging directly with the public, though the public was generally shielded by the anonymity of the talk format. Nevertheless, his manner made him popular if not even more controversial, but he was also, and perhaps unwittingly, improving his image.

In 1972 the Celtics wanted to retire his jersey and display it in the rafters of the Boston Garden with the jerseys of the many other Celtics greats, but true to form Russell refused to attend a ceremony, which frustrated both the organization and the Boston fans who still seemed at best ambivalent about Russell. Indeed, the up-roar over team president Red Auerbach's attempt to trick Russell, who by now was doing color commentary for ABC's NBA broadcasts, into attending a jersey retire-ment ceremony by scheduling it for a time when Russell would be in the Garden for a telecast ended with Russell asserting that any attempts to circumvent his wishes would end with his walking out of the arena. Thus, the jersey retirement ceremony was performed on the morning of the telecast with only former Celtic players and current team personnel present, making it vintage Russell.[16]

A televised Russell does, however, offer us a different view of the iconic former athlete, one that would combine his critical knowledge of the sport with a dry wit that he generally hid from public view up to this point. His first television broad-casting job was the three seasons he spent on the aforementioned ABC telecasts in which he would be paired with well-respected veteran play-by-play host Chris Schenkel and with whom Russell appears to have enjoyed a fine on-air relation-ship. In this capacity, Russell was able to display traits that most Americans were simply unaware of in him. First, he was honest in his appraisal of players, referees, and each game he was broadcasting. This was in marked contrast to the uncriti-cal platitudes that many color commentators offered or the vacuous commentary often given by former players. Secondly, Russell exhibited an extensive knowledge of the game complete with analyses and insight that were startling to those who saw him merely as a big man who chased rebounds and blocked shots. Russell's ability to get inside the game, as it were, and to provide perspective on the various games within the game, as they have come to be known, was a refreshing addition to the more typically trite and generally disengaged professionals working only on conjecture.

Possibly the most enjoyable display by Russell, however, was his sly sense of humor and his famous cackle of a laugh. Former players and friends had often referred to it in quiet corners and among themselves, but now the public was being made privy to it. Moreover, they liked it. By adding an air of levity to the often moribund life and death docu-dramas, as they were so often broadcast, Russell's reliance on his experiences, his scientific knowledge of the game, and his infectious laugh, some of which he would turn on himself, brought a human element to sport that was rarely present in all but the most celebrated cases. Russell didn't denigrate others; rather, he saw the humor in game situations and reminisced about his play-ing days when he himself was guilty of having done stupid things in the course of competition, and his willingness to laugh, especially at himself, made him far more endearing to the public than he had ever been before, creating in a sense a virtually new and much more favorable public persona that he would carry to a subsequent position at CBS.

In 1973 Russell agreed to return to pro basketball as the coach and general manager of the Seattle Supersonics, where he spent four relatively undistinguished seasons. Though he took a seven-year-old franchise that had been 26 and 56 the season prior and led them to the playoffs twice in four years, the Sonics won only one playoff series under Russell's leadership. For many, including Russell himself, this was unthinkable. Everywhere else he had ever been had translated into winning, but his inability to translate his on-court talent into his coaching technique somehow humanized him, and this as much as anything else, and ironically so, served to enhance his public persona. From a basketball standpoint, the biggest obstacle to Russell's success was that he did not have a Bill Russell playing for him in Seattle, something that would plague other great athletes who subsequently failed as coaches. (Ted Williams and Frank Robinson in baseball come to mind here). It has been well established that his players simply did not accept Russell's views of personal sacrifice for the good of the team as exemplified in the Celtic way. From Russell's vantage point, they were used to pampering and self-absorption; despite his efforts to the contrary, his pursuit of success and his overall manner did not resonate with that generation. From a reputation standpoint, however, and perhaps a unique quality of the American star-making machinery, his being fallible in this case afforded him the public reevaluation his constructed persona had seemingly craved from the start. In spite of the well-documented predicaments off the court, Russell had always found success on the court, but as he dealt with his first public taste of disappointment and failure with grace and humility, this version of Russell was embraced by many of the same fans and critics who had only before seen him aloof and wholly unsympathetic. From this point on, Russell's public image began to undergo a dramatic 180 degree turn. And truth be told, the Seattle team he assembled would go on to win an NBA championship two years after he left.

During the time that Russell was leading Seattle, he was elected to the Naismith Memorial Basketball Hall of Fame, but in keeping with his previous positions on individual accomplishments, he declined to attend. As always, Russell's rationale was twofold. First, the team game is not enhanced by these personal recognitions. Secondly, the Hall of Fame was racially biased in whom it did and did not enshrine.[17] This didn't endear him to a number of people, but there were those who recognized the validity, at least to a degree, of his logic. Shortly afterwards there were greater efforts made in the Hall's convoluted election process to include more outstanding African American players and coaches and contributors who had excelled outside the predominantly white basketball mainstream. This time, however, Russell's stand was not regarded as aloof but rather heroic. His struggles on the

Seattle bench had indeed opened up spaces within the public perception of Russell that had, if nothing else, allowed his actions to be finally given the benefit of the doubt and a more serious yet measured scrutiny.

Over time, Russell was honored with a number of accolades that recognized his achievements, which now grew in stature as they were viewed in historical perspective. He would also be elected to the NBA's 25th and 35th Anniversary All-Time teams while being recognized in 1995 as one of the NBA's 50 Greatest Players. Additionally, in 1980, Russell was voted the NBA's All-Time Greatest Player by the Professional Basketball Writers Association of America, though Michael Jordan appears to have wrested that title from him since.

Whatever differences writers had with Russell seem to have been either long forgotten or simply far less important than the recognition of his greatness. As a number of writers who had covered the Celtics during his playing days have either retired or died, Russell would also have a great deal less baggage to carry with him, insulating him from any unfounded criticism from a newer generation of sportswriters. Oddly enough, for those who had no firsthand knowledge of Russell as a player, he was almost universally seen as a model to be emulated while the more prickly nature of his playing days were being relegated to the dustbin of NBA history. On the other hand, the growing antipathy between writers and the entire sport media apparatus in general and the increasing black presence in the NBA also afforded Russell a boost in terms of his public persona. While in his playing days he could be considered a prime target for those weary of a black-dominated sport, the even newer Negro presence in the late twentieth-century NBA was believed to be even more problematic, as exemplified by Russell's own inability to win in Seattle and elsewhere in his coaching stops. In this regard, his once-perceived behavioral flaws were less important, and in terms of where the NBA was heading, Russell's burgeoning public persona could be viewed as less a matter of his humanity and more a matter of the lesser of two evils. Juxtaposed to the brash and well-paid modern athlete, Russell's surliness was a known quantity that in the end did little to destroy the nature of basketball and by most accounts actually enhanced it. In hindsight, thus, this reevaluation was less about Russell and more a matter of the modern athlete whose motives and behaviors challenge the status quo even more so, triggering a decidedly nostalgic embrace for the black athlete of yesteryear, an archetype for which Russell certainly fits.

CLOSING THOUGHTS

In the years following Russell's rebirth as a revered public icon, time has added to his luster. This improvement in his public persona was not a concerted effort by Russell, but came about through a combination of events and the shortness of public memory.

Interestingly, as the Celtic franchise continues to experience difficult times, even Bostonians have come to worship him, realizing what he and his style of play once meant in its context. And as they are farther and farther removed from the glory years and are no longer associated with the domination and supremacy of Russell's squad and even that of the revered Larry Bird, there is much less resentment from older fans and a more iconic following among the younger.

While these perceptions continue to change, Russell himself has softened, adding further rationale behind the more public embrace. For example, in March 1999, Russell's jersey was re-retired as part of a charitable event for the benefit of the National Mentoring Partnership and the Massachusetts Mentoring Partnership. Russell, who has become quite involved in mentoring, attended the event held at the new Fleet Center Arena in Boston and afterwards signed autographs to the delight of the young and to the shock of the older generations in attendance. In the interest of full disclosure, however, we must note here that Russell does not give his autograph away. Recognizing the recent market trends in sports memorabilia and autographs, Russell works with a collectible dealer in marketing and selling his autograph for amounts ranging from $300 to $500, but in this newer, much more forgiving climate, and perhaps amidst the antipathy of the modern fan, nobody seems to really care.

Russell has also become a popular speaker on the lecture circuit where people are exposed to his humor, insight, and sociopolitical concerns. He speaks, mostly to business groups, on leadership and motivation while being touted as the greatest winner in sport history. He even wrote a book called *11 Rules on Leadership from the Twentieth Century's Greatest Winner,* which he published in 2001.[18] His acknowledgment of those mentors who have made him successful has led him to be an active mentor of young people, which too has had an effect on his renewed public persona.

Finally, the reverence and respect with which Russell is now held was shown to basketball observers in January 2006 when NBA superstars Kobe Bryant and Shaquille O'Neal settled their infamous and longstanding feud. The impetus for that settlement was reportedly instigated by Russell himself. When cornered, O'Neal admitted: "[I] had orders from the great Bill Russell. I asked him if he ever disliked anybody he played against, and he told me, 'No, never,' and he told me that I should shake Kobe Bryant's hand and let bygones be bygones and bury the hatchet."[19] In the meantime, Russell remains a part of revered NBA basketball. He attends most NBA functions and is often used in advertising for them. Despite wearing a suit and tie, Russell is almost immediately recognizable by most fans with his distinctive gray goatee, lanky body, and sparkling eyes.

Even the NCAA has come to realize this and makes it a point of affording him ample air time whenever he attends a men's college game. Indeed, during the telecast of the 2006 NCAA Men's Division I Championship Game, he had as much camera time as retired tennis star Yannick Noah, also in attendance and whose son,

Joachim, was on the court playing for the eventual champion University of Florida Gators.

Thus, it is that Bill Russell, the former demonized player who had once come to represent the invasion of basketball by African Americans and supposed subsequent downfall, is now viewed as a basketball pioneer and a grand old man of the game. Where once he was the most controversial player as exemplified both on and off the court and one for whom the camera was rarely in focus, he has grown to become its most avid visionary, but only at a time when the fight and the youthful vigor he once displayed have been replaced by age. And while some might claim that this change is a more natural result of the country's coming to terms with bigotry and fear, an even more challenging reality is that this aging devil we know is much less threatening than the younger devils who have yet to reveal their true intentions. In this regard, Russell has become to basketball what Ali has become in a more general sense throughout the world of sport—an historically tragic figure embraced not because of the accomplishments of his youth but rather one whose presence is embraced by a culture determined to demonstrate to its youth that they themselves are incapable of traveling along a similar path without proper supervision. In this regard, a man so reviled in youth has become in his senior years a spokesperson for comportment in a sporting milieu perceived by many to be overrun with antisocial misfits and hedonists motivated solely by self-promotion.

NOTES

1. Murry Nelson, *Bill Russell, A Biography* (Westport, CT: Greenwood Press, 2005), 2.

2. Nelson, *Bill Russell*, 3.

3. Herman Masin, "Russell of Spring," *Senior Scholastic* 67, no. 14 (1 December 1956): 29.

4. Bill Russell and Taylor Branch, *Second Wind* (New York: Random House, 1979), 5.

5. No author, "Along Came Bill," *Time*, 2 January 1956: 36.

6. No author, "Not Muscle, Just Russell," *Time*, 2 April 1956: 55–56.

7. Nelson, *Bill Russell*, 6.

8. Oscar Robertson, *The Big O: My Life, My Times, My Game* (New York: Rodale Books, 2003), 63–64.

9. Frank Fitzpatrick, *"And the Walls Came Tumbling Down"* (Lincoln: University of Nebraska Press, 1999), 25–27.

10. Russell and Branch, *Second Wind*, 9.

11. Gilbert Rogin, "We Are Grown Men Playing a Child's Game," *Sports Illustrated*, 18 November 1963: 82.

12. No author, "Ol' Massa Russell," *Nation* 9 (1 March 1965): 200–211.

13. Rogin, "Grown Men," 83.

14. Edward Linn, "I Owe the Public Nothing," *Saturday Evening Post*, 18 January 1963: 60–63.

15. William F. Russell, "I'm Not Involved Anymore," *Sports Illustrated*, 16 July 1969: 18–19.

16. Russell and Branch, *Second Wind*, 12.

17. Russell and Branch, *Second Wind*, 14.

18. Bill Russell and David Falkner, *11 Rules on Leadership from the Twentieth Century's Greatest Winner* (New York: Dutton, 2001).

19. No author, "First Came a Giant Hug, Then a Lakers Victory," *New York Times*, 18 January 2006: C17.

RACING AFTER SMITH AND CARLOS

Revisiting Those Fists Some Forty Years Hence

URLA HILL

Even a Fist Was Once an Open Palm with Fingers
—Yehuda Amicha[1]

INTRODUCTION

While holding a discussion on the power of photography with a high school journalism class during the 2000–01 academic year, I pulled out the 1996 Olympic issue of *American Photographer*, which featured a color photo of San José State College sprinters Tommie Smith and John Carlos's so-called *black power* protest on the winners' podium at the 1968 Olympic Games in Mexico City.[2] I pointed out that what made photographer Ken Regan's color photo especially important was the fact that unlike the Associated Press's standard black and white version, which seems to appear whenever there is discussion on the sprinters' actions, this one allowed the audience to see that Carlos was wearing beads around his neck, and that neither Carlos nor Smith wore shoes on their feet.

In the color version of the still, it also is easier to see that Smith is holding an olive branch enclosed within a glass frame in his left hand. In contrast, the black and white AP photograph cuts off the men's legs just below each knee so that their feet are not visible while the beads around Carlos' neck and the scarf around Smith's seems to mesh hidden with the dark colors of the United States' Olympic uniform. I am guessing as well that the olive branch enclosed within a frame is barely visible because of the angle and distance from which the photographer took the picture.

I further explained to the class the various inconsistencies that continue to exist since the pair publicly expressed their disapproval of an American culture that bred discrimination amongst its citizenry. Indeed, as University of Minnesota sociologist Douglas Hartmann points out, the historical and social conditions that prompted their certainly contentious demonstration are what "account for its deeper social meaning," though, as he furthers, there are many factors that have allowed for them to be "effectively trivialized, diluted, or even erased altogether, rendering our memories of their gestures either shamelessly sentimental and meaningless on the one hand, or subject to political manipulation, reckless commercialization, and all manner of wanton co-optation on the other."[3] Hartmann also notes that the "demonstration itself remains as enigmatic and puzzling as it has been powerful and persistent."[4]

In the midst of this exceedingly teachable moment, an astute freshman informed me that he recognized the photo of Smith and Carlos from the cover of the alternative rock and roll group Rage Against the Machine's CD single "Testify." Previous students had urged me to listen to this erstwhile popular band, but somehow I just could not seem to enjoy its enraged leftist rumblings.[5] Armed with this freshly minted knowledge, however, I went in search of the aforementioned single that evening, but what I found was very much not what I would have expected. Instead of showing the medalists in black socks on the winners' podium, their AP images were cut and pasted into a body of green, red, and yellow, the colors representing the flags of several African countries as well as Guyana, South America. Their Puma running shoes, which had been strategically placed on the winners' podium in 1968, now appeared on their feet but were replaced by Adidas running shoes, a brand popularized by another alternative rock band, KORN, during the mid-1990s on the heels of the vaunted rap artists Run DMC years prior to that even.

Though the band would split up shortly after the release of "Testify" and the full-length CD *Battle of Los Angeles* in late 2000, Rage Against the Machine had promoted activism on its popular Web site that featured a segment entitled "Freedom Fighter of the Month," in which the band members note:

> Everyone has opinions on politics, social issues, and world news, but do they do anything about them? Listening to music with a radical message is only the beginning. Rage Against the Machine wants to personally acknowledge all those who are fighting for freedom in their community. One brave individual will be named the "Freedom Fighter of the Month" on the official RATM web site. RATM encourages everyone to get involved whether you are currently an activist or plan on starting now. It's time to motivate others, and Rage is giving you the opportunity to have your good work noticed.[6]

But the band never did discuss its rationale for using Smith and Carlos's image on the cover of "Testify," which forced me to surmise, right or wrong, that as with the AP photo, RATM intended the message to remain similarly obscure.

Perhaps equally as ambiguous, the AP image would appear on the back cover of the celebrated swimsuit edition of *Black Men Magazine* in August 2006. The black and white photo appears in an ad for the rap artist Saigon and sits atop a letter from the Department of Justice that is stamped "ARMED AND DANGEROUS." I am guessing that its intent is to offer a more positive representation given that the fictional character who adorns the storyline, Che Johnson, has only been accused of "educating the community and empowering the urban community through knowledge and respect of self-advocating social and political awareness, and economic empowerment in the black and Latino communities."[7]

Regardless, it would appear that the vaunted image of Smith and Carlos seems to fit in many different contexts these days, which in many ways seems to beg more questions than it answers. Thus, when the now San José State University announced that it was preparing to erect a twenty-foot statue to honor Smith and Carlos for their courageous stand on the Olympic dais in 1968, I was apprehensive, to say the least. Initially, I questioned the institution's ability to promote and ultimately present a worthwhile discussion of these sprinters' collective actions given the myriad interpretations, misinterpretations, controversies, and such that have long since surrounded the moment. Predictably, this has already been the case given that the statue's very presence has already been sucked into those tautological, seemingly endless loops of supposition that continue to weigh heavy on both the actors, the principals, their supporters, and their adversaries alike, especially as the discussion moves further into debates regarding black militancy and rage that remains all too prevalent all these years since.

To be sure, the sprinters' activities, which really boil down to the raising of those gloved fists, continues to bring about questions regarding the pair's intentions relative to the public's consciousness—then and now. As John Carlos himself pointed out in a 2001 article, the American public largely remains frightened by their actions that day in Mexico City. Smith would too note that it was always "the fist that scared people. . . . White folks would have forgiven the black socks, the silk scarf, the bowed head. But they saw that raised black fist and were afraid."[8] On a personal note, I still find that Smith and Carlos were correct in their assumptions, but while the clenched fists continue to garner the most attention still, one fact has changed decidedly: Smith and Carlos have ascended their place as villainous traitors to become a sort of brand for gallantry and pluck in the face of inestimable odds, and it is in this regard that the aforementioned statue is merely one aspect of this push to revitalize or even give the moment a more modern measure of perspective as well as a decidedly more contemporary level of clarity. Thus, purely in the context of the fêted Smith and Carlos moment, these actions, actions that have remained as incontrovertible as they most assuredly have remained controversial, have borne a remarkable transformation of late, one that seems poised to both redeem and perhaps, to borrow from Hartmann, diminish their place in American cultural history.[9]

CONSTRUCTING A CULTURE OF PROTEST

The lead-up to the Smith and Carlos moment during the 1968 Summer Olympics is a complex and multifaceted matter, to be sure. Still, its evolutionary character is as intriguing as the gestures themselves and warrants a more proper fleshing out in terms of tracing the changing nature of public perception of their collective actions.

Indeed, the moment itself grew out of a movement that had begun to evolve as the result of situations arising at San José State College. Initially, this movement, which went through several incarnations, as noted below, seemed to be just another assemblage amidst the cacophony of the age itself, but following some initial growing pains, it festered into a full-service movement that incorporated as well as mirrored the turbulence of the times and fought for lasting change both within and without the San José community.

One of the more significant and certainly motivating events that took place on the campus in the months prior to the 1968 Games was the threat of a boycott by the college's black football players before their game against the University of Texas at El Paso (UTEP) late in 1967. It had long been known that the UTEP football program was clearly discriminatory in that black players were not recruited to play for the football team in spite of the great advances made by Coach Don Haskins's basketball program that had recently won the NCAA championship with an all-black starting line-up.[10] Notwithstanding that success, and as remained more typical to the times, all roads to progress in collegiate sport led through football, which lent a sense of urgency to the planned action. As San José State's own Harry Edwards, the one figure in the middle of most of what would transpire in the months to come, recalls, the threat of the protest turning violent allowed the protestors to win out, leading to the cancellation of the game, but it was not without a cost, financial and otherwise, to the college and the observably conservative community.[11] Still, and if nothing else, San José State's black students, and especially the more in-sync black student athletes, had learned that there was some room to exploit the elites' poorly concealed lust for sport by attacking them at their most vulnerable points.[12]

For Edwards, the significance of the UTEP protest can be found in the fact that it brought together en masse the small but increasingly vocal numbers of nonwhite students and supporters while bringing along with it as well a sense of purpose rarely seen in this regard. More importantly, as Edwards would note, this demonstrated the value of harnessing athletics "as a lever to bring about social, academic and political changes at an educational institution."[13] Indeed, the success of the black students' protest quickly led to several improvements on campus, including a broad based antidiscrimination policy that was to include issues relative to housing as well as the fraternities and sororities and the creation of a special college officer—an ombudsman—whose primary purpose was to monitor and oversee matters construed as discriminatory.[14] It also brought a momentum to what had been a staggering and certainly ineffective period for San José State's minorities.

Hartmann notes that the accomplishments of what would develop into the United Black Students for Action (UBSA) on the San José State campus were regularly ignored and even denigrated in some fashion by the press, but he also claims that the sporting arena at San José State, as it more than likely would have been on any other college campus during that time period, had proven to be one of the "most important and concrete arenas of contention."[15] Hartmann continues that while the cancellation of the UTEP game served as an integral tool for aspiring campus activists, its effect for Smith, Carlos, and Lee Evans, the third but typically most overlooked member of the track and field team's active triumvirate, would be virtually immeasurable.[16] As Smith himself would note, the actions taken in regard to UTEP football "forced me to read and think about the problems of this day and age—even more than 6 months ago."[17] This would give rise to a simmering antiestablishment movement that sought to reclaim and reposition sport in the most general sense while giving rise to an increasingly more fashionable move toward politicizing the Olympic Games in a much more broadly conceived fashion, one that would ultimately bring the newly infused character of American civil disobedience to a world rather than merely a national stage.

HARRY EDWARDS

Certainly another key component toward a more critical understanding of what was happening in and around the San José State campus at the time would be Harry Edwards. Candid and outspoken, Edwards had played basketball and threw the discus as an undergraduate in the early 1960s and was certainly as personally vested in what would take place as any other person involved, but upon his return to the campus in 1967, he would emerge as a bold force for change as evinced by both his teaching and his equally compelling activist work.

The extent to which Edwards remains enigmatic, to say the least, and especially in the context of the various countercultural challenges of the day, can be found in the wide speculation and various opinions of him that would find their way into the mainstream consciousness once he reemerged on campus following his foray to graduate school. For example, the late Pete Axthelm, writing in *Sports Illustrated* and using the heated and certainly contentious New York Athletic Club track and field event boycott in February 1968 as a backdrop, introduced the deeply entrenched Edwards, a key organizer of the New York action, as an increasingly more dynamic leader, the sort of compelling force who demonstrated that he could both organize and carry out high-profile acts of civil disobedience, though publicly he would come to be regarded as a much more condescending and even dangerous figure. In contrast, former San José State president, Robert D. Clark, as much a friend to the nascent activism taking shape as there would be on his campus, was initially pleased with Edwards's obvious leadership qualities and his ability to negotiate for the betterment of blacks as admirable traits, but he would also note that Edwards's more admirable (read here palatable in the mainstream) qualities "are hidden by the fact that he is also a fiery militant," a virtually ill-defined but ubiquitous though quite powerful term in its own right. Clark would further contend that in spite of Edwards's leadership qualities, he could easily coerce the masses, suggesting that his "unrestrained denunciation of whites, his angry threats or warnings, his towering presence" intimidated whites while evoking a passionate and certainly antagonistic response that Clark contends complicates the problem of appraisal rather than aid the cause. This, Clark believed, was made even more problematic in that in their entirety, Edwards's actions, alongside his confrontational behavior and demeanor, were "unbecoming of a college teacher."[18]

For Edwards, however, the reputation-related issues seemed then as well as now to be much less consequential, especially in light of the gathering storm that would mark 1968. Indeed, Edwards claims that when he arrived on the San José State campus during the fall of 1966, he sported three-piece suits while acting the part of the 1960s-era buttoned-down college professor. After all, he had just returned from graduate school at Cornell University, a campus shrouded in an Ivy League setting, and was now preparing to teach on a college campus. Upon his return to campus, Edwards, along with Ken Noel, a former distance runner who was pursuing an advanced degree at SJS, established that "the same social and racial injustices and discrimination that had dogged [their] footsteps as freshman in San José were still rampant on campus—racism in the fraternities and sororities, racism in housing, racism and out-and-out mistreatment in athletics, and a general lack of understanding of the problems of *Afro*-Americans by the college administration."[19] With a newly minted sense of race consciousness emerging around them that acted as a sort of catalyst, Edwards retired those three-piece suits and developed the sort of combative bearing that he would contend became a feeding frenzy for mainstream media but with very mixed results.[20]

While reacquainting himself with the San José State culture, Edwards, and again in partnership with Noel and the range of student supporters who would ultimately form the aforementioned USBA, fought relentlessly for equality in every aspect of campus life. Through hearings, rallies, protests, and continued sparring with the local press, they were able to force changes in the college administration's policies. So when Edwards helped initiate and ultimately pilot the charge for black athletes to boycott the 1968 Olympic Games, he had long since demonstrated his capacity to front such a feat, a matter certainly not lost among USOC officials who had demonstrated both a deep and abiding concern about such unrest and an equally deep and abiding dislike for Edwards himself. Nevertheless, and while controversy rages on—then as well as now—Edwards played a primary role in organizing the proposed boycott and ultimately shaping the attitudes and outlooks of the athletes who eventually went on to Mexico City filled with the spirit of active agency.

THE OLYMPIC PROJECT FOR HUMAN RIGHTS

According to Kevin B. Witherspoon of Lander University in South Carolina, the debate of the merits of boycotting the Olympic Games on discriminatory grounds began as early as 1960. He cites Olympic gold-medallist Rafer Johnson, who noted that discussions had taken place over a possible action that would have targeted the Rome games scheduled for that summer. Witherspoon further notes the efforts of comedian and activist Dick Gregory, a former distance runner at Southern Illinois University in Carbondale who spent time at San José State during the late sixties, as the man who had initially suggested a boycott of those Games. He would later take up the same charge in regard to the Tokyo Games in 1964.[21]

While Gregory's proposal received very little support among Olympians at that time, once black athletes arrived in Tokyo and found themselves in the familiar role of a second-class citizenry, as witnessed by many of their assignments and accommodations, many were prompted to rethink these previous propositions, though ultimately any such plans were put on the back burner. From then on, however, and as Witherspoon would note, "At every major track meet that followed the games, Black athletes got together and talked about the possibility of a Black boycott of the 1968 Olympics,"[22] though these initial discussions lacked the sort of organizational expertise that would later emerge in the run-up to 1968 through the efforts of Edwards and others.[23]

To be sure, and certainly in contrast to the previous calls for such collective actions, the 1967 appeal for what would become the Olympic Project for Human Rights (OPHR), spearheaded by Edwards, would take on a life of its own. In many ways the OPHR can be viewed as a sort of stylized and highly proficient cross between Gregory's aforementioned attempts to organize black athletes and a now forward-moving USBA that was poised to extend its reach beyond the confines of the San José campus and its surrounding environs and enter into a much more nationalized fray as evidenced by the platform Edwards carved out in a 1967 rally on the SJS campus. These proposals called for, among other things:

• The restoration of Muhammad Ali's title and right to box in this country.
• The removal of the anti-Semitic and antiblack Avery Brundage from his post as Chairman of the International Olympic Committee.
• A curtailment of participation of all-white teams and individuals from the Union of South Africa and Southern Rhodesia in all United States and Olympic Athletic events.
• The addition of at least two black coaches to the men's track and field coaching staff appointed to coach the 1968 United States Olympic team.
• The appointment of at least two black people to policymaking positions on the United States Olympic Committee.
• The complete desegregation of the bigot-dominated and racist New York Athletic Club.[24]

During the rally, Edwards, who seemed to be growing bolder with each passing advance, also made it clear that the ramifications of not meeting these initiatives would prove problematic for authority, demonstrating above all else that the strategy behind the protests was to take full advantage of the one area where a minority presence had some momentum. As Edwards recalls in his seminal *The Revolt of the Black Athlete*:

> First of all, we recognized something that perhaps the casual observer did not—that athletics was, in fact, as racist as any other areas of college life. Second, we felt that we had to utilize a power lever that would bring the community and student body as well as the administration of the college into the pressure situation. We had seen, all too often, the spectacle of black people demonstrating and picketing groups, organizations, and institutions of limited concern to people in positions of power. We therefore decided to use something more central to the concerns of the entire local community structure—athletics.[25]

But not everyone could be so easily persuaded. Edwards had problems recruiting athletes early on in the movement, with three-time Olympian Ralph Boston and the aforementioned two-time Olympian Rafer Johnson both voicing their displeasure after the initial meeting that took place at the Black Youth Conference on November 22 and 23, 1967, in Los Angeles. Boston, who captured a gold medal (1960), a silver (1964), and a bronze (1968) in the long jump, was apparently unimpressed with Edwards's collegiate athletic capabilities or any of the other great minds believing in what appeared to some as a worthwhile project, claiming that the "whole thing has been picked up by people who are not athletes."[26] He also echoed the sentiments of the majority of the American populace in declaring that politics should not intersect with sport, which remained a potent force late into the civil rights era in spite of events to come. And Johnson, a silver (1956) and gold (1960) medallist in the decathlon, cried out in a similar fashion that the "Olympic Committee has always been fair to the Negro."[27]

Neither Boston nor Johnson, however, though both highly respected among the committee and teammates alike, would hold the same sway as would the iconic Jesse Owens, who through 1968 at least would remain as respected a figure as there was in the USOC. Interestingly enough, Owens, who claimed four gold medals at the 1936 Berlin Games, and other black athletes who had made the American team that year had an opportunity to boycott the so-called "Nazi Games," as they came to be called, but they opted to compete anyway, a decision made in the face of Jewish American boycotts and one that would later prove to be flawed.[28] Regardless, Owens unflinchingly believed that there was "no place in the athletic world for politics" and that the Olympic Games "helped bridge the gap of misunderstanding of people."[29] And though these voices maintained their hold over the majority of the American athletic contingent, those who advocated for stronger language and action continued to chip away at the decidedly conservative facade long since erected.

Nevertheless, and unlike others within the various movements, Edwards had established clearly marked goals while aligning himself with other movements in play elsewhere around the country. In fact, he noted that active participants in the movement decided to bring on as many recognized leaders as possible including Dr. Martin Luther King, Jr., and Floyd McKissick, director of the Congress of Racial Equality (CORE). Edwards would also contact newly ascended Student Non-Violent Coordinating Committee leader H. Rap Brown, who came aboard during the abovementioned boycott of the New York Athletic Club.[30] Thus, it would be through what had begun as more localized efforts that Edwards and others would begin to foment much larger strides in combating period race prejudice, all of which was designed specifically to take on the prevailing racialized climate found within and without the whole of American sport, which would then find its widest audience in the lead up to the 1968 Summer Games. And though the boycott idea ultimately fizzled, the notion of individuals conducting individual acts of defiance, subtle though they may have been, had been firmly planted into the culture of the team, and when coupled with the already intense political climate that had gripped Mexico City that summer, all signs pointed to a combustible program in the offing.

THE GESTURES IN THEIR CONTEXT

In spite of the remarkable exhibition of athletic artistry displayed by the American team throughout the 1968 Summer Games, it is no stretch to conclude that the most indelibly etched impression of those particular weeks took place on the medal dais following the 200 meter sprint. The sight of Smith and Carlos with their fists raised in the air, a stance that eclipsed—almost humorously so—silver medallist's Peter Norman's OPHR badge that dangled boldly from his sweatshirt, in many ways served as the formal pronouncement that the heretofore passive black presence in American sport would be no longer, and that the age of the so-called new black athlete, politically grounded, resolute, and aware of both the past and the present, had arrived. Of course this message would be challenged in some very public arenas that sought to discredit and ultimately devalue the work of the OPHR and others as the work of unpatriotic and petulant scoundrels, which is how we can best account for the remarkable backlash and sustained animus toward what transpired.

For the most part, the furor that erupted as a result of the Smith/Carlos moment came about over the symbolism related to the fist at a time when the fist was undergoing a sort of renaissance as a tool of protest, most notably at the time in regard to the members of the Black Panther Party. To be candid, it is important to note that the fist has a unique and storied history, crossing centuries, continents, connotations, and cultures. As Gottfried Korff, Professor for Empirical Cultural Sciences at the Eberhard Karl University in Tübingen, Germany, notes, the use of the clenched fist has long been used as a humanizing symbol, a symbol of "binding loyalty to a social-political cause" that serves as a "readily recognizable political" sign while aiding groups in forming a sense of "consciousness through internal self-identification and demarcation from other groups."[31] Now whether the gesture has retained what Professor Gottfried insists is a significance that dates as far back as the sixteenth century is perhaps beyond the scope of this analysis. Still, it is important to note here that during the 1960s, and in addition to the Black Panthers, the most recognizable and perhaps even feared of those era organizations that would adopt the symbolism, the fist had made numerous appearances in posters and fliers for various political activities, which includes the more typically white American Communist Party. The raised fist also served as a symbol for such diverse organizations as the National Organization of Women, the American Indian Movement, the Movimiento Estudiantil Chicano de Aztlan, the United Farm Workers of America, and even the Weathermen, the more radical offshoot of the Students for a Democratic Society, whose members—with the exception of the latter—all adopted variations of the nonviolent principles of Mahatma Gandhi and Dr. King.

Indeed, the raised fist is no stranger some forty years after Smith and Carlos. As recently as the 2005 season, the international athletic governing body for soccer, Fédération Internationale de Football Association (FIFA), sanctioned player Paolo di Canio for a series of raised-arm salutes during competition for fear that it might possibly provoke a violent reaction from fans and players alike.[32] Nevertheless, and as is the case when it comes to Nazi swastikas, Smith and Carlos's black-gloved fists, associated as they have become with the Black Panther Party, evoked such fear that the resulting backlash against them seems against today's backdrop to have been entirely misplaced and certainly driven by panic more than rational concern. Thus, while the moment was by both sprinters' accounts intended to be peaceful in its form, the image of the victors raising of their black-gloved fists represented violence in the minds of many Americans, something that was not necessarily lost on the athletes themselves. For example, Smith recalls that once Carlos and he shot their fists into the air, the stadium grew so quiet that he could hear both the wind circling his fist and Lee Evans muttering "Oh shit!" from a distance,[33] a sentiment that seems to operate in a variety of directions. In contrast to the uncertainty uttered in the Evans expletive was the staunch dressing-down of journalists such as Brent Musburger, currently one of America's most beloved sport commentators, who the next day referred to Smith and Carlos as "black-skinned storm troopers"[34] in the pages of the *Chicago American*.

Thus again, the key to the brewing controversy can be found in the reactions of those who assumed that a raised fist was a symbol of an ill-defined yet presumed violent call to actual, as opposed to metaphoric, arms. As Hartmann concedes, the concept of black power, as it emanated from the various corners of mainstream thought, demonstrated both a positive as well as a negative subtext and could vary between a political stand, an emergent racialist philosophy, or perhaps even a combination of the two, which could be a terrifying thought to those whose conceptual underpinning had been a decidedly alarmist and racist mainstream press.[35] While neither Smith nor Carlos ever demonstrated a penchant or even an attraction to violence—then as well as now—they were certainly systematically tarred with that particular brush, which left them to suffer a level of public indignation not typically associated with such a muted form of protest. On the other hand, given the propensity for over-reaction that so marks that age, the inevitability of finding the sort of overarching link to supposed violence proved too powerful an attraction, and, subsequently, the initial move to connect the gesture not with a more integrated (read less outwardly aggressive) civil rights movements but rather with an emergent form of black rage, as generally couched in the discussion of the Black Panther Party, proved to make for a rather unsophisticated association. Nevertheless, the link to a supposed militancy would underscore the moment, one that would continue to inform all sides of the discussion from several differing angles as the debate raged forward.

BLACK POWER

Another factor in most of the lingering disquiet can also be found in that many linked the twin-fisted gestures to the nascent yet rapidly escalating black power movement. It should be noted here that a black power movement included political ideologies from a vast array of intellectuals ranging from Stokely Carmichael, who is typically credited with coining the phrase, to Angela Davis, Ron Karenga, Malcolm X, and Huey Newton, for example. Although their strategies and philosophies within this so-deemed movement differed, they shared a common goal, which was to bring about a strong and unifying sense of racial identity amongst African Americans.

Indeed, it is little wonder that so many Americans persist in linking Smith and Carlos's action to militancy. As Martin Duberman explains in his essay "Black Power and the American Radical Tradition (1968),"[36] the simplistic phrase "black power" has been a source for national dismay for a variety of reasons that include language, which more often than not are contextually driven by agendas and various forms of ideological baggage. Furthermore, as Duberman points out, complicated terminologies, attitudes, or phenomena are simplified to symbols, which offer a range of interpretive moments. Thus, for Duberman, black power is an ambiguous phrase that has been mishandled by its proponents, who offer "different defini-tions on different occasions, in part because their own understanding of the term continues to develop, but in part, too, because their explanations have been tailored to their audiences. The confusion has been compounded by the press, which has frequently distorted the words of SNCC and CORE representatives, harping on every connotation of violence and reverse racism, minimizing the central call for racial unity."[37]

The philosophy of black power is thus a blend of varied, and in part compet-ing, elements, and it cannot be predicted with any certainty that the phrase will assume dominance. In this regard, Smith and Carlos's pose has historically been relegated to a more brazen, i.e. public, form of black power symbolism, and given their physical proximity to the epicenter of the Black Panther movement, Oakland, California, and its surrounding municipalities, it is little wonder that so many had and continue to assign it a Panther-inspired bearing all these years hence.

What becomes even more challenging for those who sought to read the gestures as they were intended was what appeared to be an overlapping of many of these disparate groups that gave rise to latent fears that black America was organizing itself against the whole of the country. This was especially true given the genuine lack of accountability on the part of a mainstream press that seemed to be working in conjunction with those bodies aiming to first discredit and ultimately destroy any semblance of what can best be described as the momentum for antiracism initiatives and activism.

There existed concomitant confusion that black power as a trend was somehow aligned with what were conceived to be the more overtly violent-prone groups, and most specifically the Black Panther Party, which remained the most controversial yet certainly misunderstood organization in the mix. As Wesleyan University professor Algernon Austin would point out in a paper presented before the 2003 American Sociological Association convention, even many prominent period scholars failed to place the black power struggle within the larger framework of period civil rights. For Austin, thus, if the academic community was having difficulties separating violence from those emergent efforts at building grassroot platforms, what chance would the general population have given that much of its information about such matters came from an unsympathetic press.[38] Or as Peniel E. Joseph notes in *Waiting 'til the Midnight Hour: A Narrative History of Black Power in America*, many Americans saw the move away from Martin Luther King Jr.'s "hopeful rhetoric toward [a] polemics of black nationalists who blamed whites for the worsening urban crisis" as a step backwards while pointing to the "gun-toting Black Panthers who vowed to lead a political revolution with an army of the black underclass"[39] as the most logical outcome of such a shift.

In his impacting critique of that summer's events, sociologist Douglas Hartmann brings up a range of intriguing points in regard to the public's reaction to black power while juxtaposing it with the Smith and Carlos moment. He notes, for example, that while the mainstream tended to, in general, claim a measure of compassion for the plight of the black man in America, many would also conclude that Smith and Carlos's assault on American racism was ill conceived and ill advised in terms of its form, i.e. the fist; its timing, i.e. during the anthem; and its airing out of national matters on a worldwide stage, i.e. the unspoken practice of keeping politics from the games. Moreover, given the move away from the earlier tactics toward a more modern approach infused with the notion of black power, antiracism initiatives could be posed as a clarion call for a violent response. Thus, in further investigating the reaction to the events in Mexico City, as Hartmann rightly suggests, lost in the translation between the mainstream and along the periphery was the character and form that protest might take in this regard. He notes that the largely white American base was caught unaware of the subtlety behind the gestures and later statements regarding race in the United States, leaving many Americans, despite their political leanings, to conclude that their gestures were a symbol of racial violence as of yet unrealized but imminent, which in 1968 was considered to be a much more likely event given the spate of rioting in Watts, Cleveland, Newark, Detroit, and elsewhere.[40]

Addressing this controversy head on, however, Harry Edwards would assign a much more structured, and hence predictable reading of the form that the public's reaction had assumed. Edwards noted the media's continued insistence that Smith and Carlos's gestures were linked to the Black Panther Party and its assumed militancy, which he first rejected and then subsequently inverted by referring to their action repeatedly as a "Black Dignity salute."[41] As he notes in the foreword of his *The Revolt of the Black Athlete*: "At the University of New Mexico during the 1968–69 basketball season black students marched onto the gym floor and gave the Black Dignity salute—dramatized by Tommie Smith and John Carlos during the 1968 Olympic Games—while the national anthem was being played just prior to the beginning of a U.N.M.-Brigham Young University basketball contest."[42]

Edwards's apprehension toward seeing the gesture within the more broadly conceived black power motif was certainly understandable. At the time it contained a wealth of loaded symbolism that appeared poised to bring forth images of the more egregious aspects of an era that had grown accustomed to a more decorous civil rights movement. Either way, Edward's observations remain the most levelheaded in terms of the significance and meaning many read into the gestures themselves, which, if one can believe either Smith or Carlos, were never intended to be anything other than a silent call for equality, a matter that bears further scrutiny, especially as it pertains to the legacy and the treatment the two athletes received following their expulsion from the Olympic Village.

THE BLACK PANTHER CONNECTION

Certainly the last word in the debate surrounding this controversial Olympic moment is the supposition that Smith and Carlos were demonstrating above all else that they were either in league with or actively sympathetic to the Black Panther cause, something that has been proven fallacious in the years since the 1968 Summer Games. For example, according to Dr. Jeffrey O. G. Ogbar, director of the Institute for African American Studies at the University of Connecticut, it would be unlikely that the Black Panther Party would have shown that much interest in the sort of muted political protest offered by Smith and Carlos that afternoon. The party faithful had certainly refused to buy into much of what had become acceptable for the masses of participants within what they maintained was a more docile and certainly made-for-mainstream general movement. Thus, while many black power–oriented groups worked from the *black is beautiful* motif made popular by the late 1960s while expressing themselves through pan-Africanist behaviors and fashions, including the wearing of dashikis and either braided or natural hairstyles, a more typical Panthers' uniform consisted of a black leather jacket, a powder blue shirt, black shoes, black pants, and black berets, inspired by films of the French resistance during the Second World War.[43] They also carried other not-quite-fashionable accessories during the era, i.e. loaded pistols, shotguns, and assault rifles in order to better monitor the activity of the police in predominately black neighborhoods while protecting themselves and their neighbor/supporters.

Interestingly enough, during the Mexico City Games, Carlos was pictured standing next to teammate and former Winston-Salem State University hurdler Leon Coleman, who was in African-inspired attire rather than black leather and a powder blue shirt. And following the Games, Smith and Carlos appeared in dashikis while touring various campuses, hardly the makings of a Panther-like manifestation.[44] As Ogbar would note, "In many ways, the Panthers didn't understand the beauty of Black people seeing themselves with natural hair and affirming themselves in ways that Blacks hadn't experienced,"[45] making it even less likely that either scenario—Smith and Carlos were Panthers or the Panthers were moving toward a more public and palpably pop-cultural display—was close to accurate depictions.

Though they existed some years prior, the Panthers burst onto the national scene on May 2, 1967, at a time when many black Americans began to question Martin Luther King's nonviolence stance. That afternoon, twenty-six members of the party showed up on the steps of the California State Capitol in Sacramento in protest of the state legislature's hearing on gun-control legislation, known as the Mulford Act, which the media referred to as the "Panther Bill." Introduced by ultraconservative assemblyman Don Mulford and signed into law by another ultraconservative, then California Governor Ronald Reagan, the Mulford Act was a direct response to the Panthers' patrolling of the police. By that one evening, the Black Panthers became better known by the fairly ubiquitous refrain as "the Negroes with guns" as their images popped up on television screens across America and around the world.

In actuality, the Black Panthers offered an alternative that seemed to both attract and frighten a number of African Americans—probably from the expected fallout alone[46]—and certainly countless mainstream whites. Unlike the many other groups that emerged during the era, they were more typically noted for the casualties that came about as a result of shootouts with law enforcement. Even more to the point, they did not believe that the African-inspired names and dashikis could underscore the struggle itself, and, thus, they sought more direct means to engage with the public and seemed to revel in the ways that they could rattle an increasingly soporific populace. On this point alone, Dr. King, certainly skeptical of such tactics himself, was nonetheless moved to observe:

So Black Power is now a part of the nomenclature of the national community. To some it is abhorrent, to others dynamic; to some it is repugnant, to others exhilarating; to some it is destructive, to others it is useful. Since Black Power means different things to different people and indeed, being essentially an emotional concept, can mean different things to the same person on differing occasions, it is impossible to attribute its ultimate meaning to any single individual or organization. One must look beyond personal styles, verbal flourishes and the hysteria of the mass media to assess its values, its assets, and liabilities honestly.[47]

Perhaps the confusion over whether or not Edwards, Carlos, Smith, and the other black athletes were linked to the Black Panthers began in the aftermath of Dr. King's assassination in April 1968. In those chaotic days following King's murder, an angered Edwards held a press conference announcing that he was poised to join the Black Panther Party and encouraged other black professionals to join similarly more combative groups in order to help serve notice that American society could no longer sit idly by while important black figures were being gunned down with impunity. Additionally, Edwards, who held press conferences at the offices of the San Francisco *Sun-Reporter*, a black publication, and at nearby Stanford University, noted that Black America was being backed into a corner by such overtly violent tactics, and, thus, even if individual men and women did not agree with the proposed goals of the Black Panther Party, there were virtually no alternatives to taking on a similar posture. As he would note, channeling yet another late black leader, "We shall overcome, yes. But I want to add one more stanza: by any means necessary."[48] He would further emphasize his exasperation by exclaiming, "I personally encourage violence, until somebody shows me a better way. Non-violence essentially has not worked."[49]

Local columnist Dick Hallgren likely added to the tension when he described Edwards's tone as "impassioned, sarcastic, sorrowful, angry, anguished, and finally desperate."[50] Yet, while Edwards had taken such a public stand in the months leading up to the Mexico City Games, none of the San José State sprinters had assumed such a position nor had any of the other OPHR converts training in the Sierras publicly espoused such a plan.[51] Moreover, and to be quite frank on this point, it seems unlikely that the Black Panther Party itself would have put all that much effort into such a relatively passive and certainly muted protest in spite of the attention it received and the resultant public recoil. Nevertheless, given the visual alone, and especially when coupled with the Panthers' propensity for thrusting black-gloved fists in the air, there is little doubt that the combination of a visibly well-armed Black Panther Party frightening the already heightened masses would complicate matters for Smith and Carlos.

Even the renowned President Clark may have lent some further life to the increasingly apocryphal reports. Though he was rumored to have been forced out of office for supporting Smith and Carlos's efforts, he, nonetheless, referred to their protest as the "Black Panther salute" in an article that he wrote in 1988.[52]

There is also little doubt that J. Edgar Hoover, the former director of the Federal Bureau of Investigation (FBI), added to the American public's fear of the Panthers and by extension Smith and Carlos too, for that matter. Although the Black Panthers did not appear on the FBI's initial list of targeted Black Nationalist Hate Groups in August of 1967, by September of 1968, just weeks before Smith and Carlos's remonstrations in Mexico City, Hoover would declare the Black Panthers the preeminent threat to the country's internal security. The FBI's counterintelligence program (COINTELPRO), in operation between 1956 and 1971, had directed its agents to expose, disrupt, misdirect, and discredit politically radical and dissident political organizations from King's Southern Christian Leadership Conference to the American Nazi Party to the Ku Klux Klan. But by the mid-1960s, agents' efforts were redirected to focus on black power groups, with 233 of its 295 operations directed against the Panthers alone. Perhaps more than any other factor, this thread would place Smith and Carlos officially alongside Huey Newton, Bobby Seale, Fred Hampton, and the others caught up in the COINTELPRO operation and would offer further credence to the notion that what these two young men had on their mind that afternoon in Mexico City was not freedom but mayhem, the most enduring myth of the entire episode.

Interestingly, neither Smith nor his former fellow activist with the UBSA Lee Evans had ever claimed a link to the Panthers. In fact, there is no mistaking Smith's or Evans' feelings about being linked to the Panthers or any of the other so-called militant organizations which they were systematically said to have fronted. As Smith and Evans would both acknowledge in 2003, they generally found Panther tactics to conflict with each other's personal belief systems,[53] a point Smith would all but concede in an interview given the day following the actual protest on the podium when he explained to renowned ABC Sports commentator Howard Cosell: "My raised right hand stood for the power in Black America. Carlos's raised left hand stood for the unity of Black America. Together they formed an arch of unity and power. The black scarf around my neck stood for Black pride in racist America. The totality of our effort was the regaining of Black dignity."[54] Fresh on his mind and likely in no mood to tread lightly, given that Carlos and he had already been expelled from the Olympic Village, Smith's explanation seems as plausible today as it was ostensibly ignored then.

REDEMPTION THROUGH ARTISTIC ENTERPRISE

Irrespective of the persistent conjecture over whether the moment was couched in the militant imagery of black power or that it was intended to be a peaceful, reflective show of dissent, the fact is that these many years removed, the image of that dual pose remains one of, if not the most, memorable moments in modern American sport history. It is also a moment, interestingly enough, that is typically discussed in the present tense, and nowhere is this view more substantiated than

The above statue, unveiled in October 2005, was organized by San José State University graduate Erik Grotz to commemorate the activism of 1968 Olympians and fellow Spartans Tommie Smith and John Carlos. Courtesy, History San José.

in the decision to erect a monument to Smith and Carlos in the heart of the since renamed San José State University campus.

Certainly, the decision to erect such a shrine is in and of itself an extraordinarily telling accomplishment. Unveiled on the thirty-seventh anniversary of the duo's controversial exploits and designed by the acclaimed Bay-area sculptor Rigo 23, the bronze statue stands across from Clark Hall, named in honor of the former San José State College president who supported the black athletes in their advocacy efforts regardless of the very public beating he took as a result. Still, and perhaps even more significant, it has come with expenditures far and away exceeding the actual dollar amounts inherent to the project.

One consequence of all this is that it has once again led to a renewal of local, regional, and even national debates as to what happened in 1968, how the moment came to be, and why it all mattered in the first place. Now whether or not this is simply a matter of merely addressing or even redressing old wounds is by itself fascinating, and it has certainly accomplished that.

Additionally, the hoopla surrounding the statue's unveiling has led to the restoration of several all but ignored, though no less substantial, legacies to the San

José campus. Indeed, and in spite of the efforts of Dr. Clark and his initial choice for the dual role of ombudsman and race-relations counselor, J. Benton White, a white minister who happened to hail from Birmingham, Alabama, and who was appointed in order to help diffuse the racial tension that existed on campus, Smith and Carlos and really even Harry Edwards and Lee Evans had all been virtually erased from the institution's public face, though to this day they remain the institution's most recognizable, if not infamous, markers. This, of course, all gives rise to yet another extraordinary development in the entire narrative, specifically what it all means some forty years since, which certainly begs the question: How can such a vilified and certainly controversial moment find rejuvenation if not outright rehabilitation under the guise of an entirely different context? True, this moment might have occurred in Mexico City, and, yes, it happened nearly forty years ago, but from the start it was apparent that what begun a world away was the material face of what was happening nationally, regionally, and locally—specifically San José—around a much more blatantly contentious struggle for change.

This monument would also serve to resurrect the criticism of the moment while also serving to force a reevaluation of where things have gone all these years hence. It exposed the architects—principal or peripheral—of both the dedication and the moment itself to some fairly potent scrutiny from both within as well as from outside the campus community. Now, evidently, whether or not these extraordinary events can be contained within the language of a more substantive move toward progress or whether they are merely a snapshot of the sort of cynical nod toward race relations that marks an age dedicated to tolerance rather than the eradication of bigotry and one that prefers platitudes to substantive change remains to be seen and is certainly being explored on and off campus. Nevertheless, the reawakening of this once sleeping giant is in and of itself symptomatic of a community still awed by how to recognize, let alone interpret, such an event, especially when what goes for modern Olympic-styled protest today is the sort of preening and prancing around in American flags as could be found by U.S. sprinters during the 2000 Sydney Olympics so decried by Tommie Smith.[55] Thus in this respect, the more substantive work of making sense of the shift from shame to celebration is a key to discovering the context within which this sculpture lies today.

One integral sign of this would have to be the discussion of the monument on the San José State campus. To be sure, while the university has received some quite positive letters following the initial announcement and ultimately the dedication of the statue, it has too received letters of outrage. Thus, while a Clayton, North Carolina, resident could note her pleasure with the university's efforts on behalf of Smith and Carlos, noting that she had hopes the "memorial will stand as a testament to their courage and bravery for many generations to come,"[56] there were others who saw things from a fundamentally different orientation altogether, a sampling of which can be found below:[57]

June 27, 2005

Alumni Director:

I am furious. I came very close to not sending in this renewal. I am totally embarrassed by the actions of the University to Honor the dishonorable actions of the two athletes in the Mexico Olympics. Please share my (our) gross displeasure with the Administration of what once was a proud institution.

• • •

October 18, 2005

Mr. Selter:[58]

I was absolutely astonished to read in *USA Today* that SJSU had erected and dedicated a statue to Smith and Carlos.

Those individuals were an outright embarrassment as representatives of their country. The Olympics has never been a place for politics, but these two morons decided it was, and it was outrageously shameful. I do not deny them their right to speak their minds . . . however, there is a time and a place, and the Olympics wasn't it. Adolf Hitler, Jimmy Carter, and the Palestinians all thought politics should play a role in the Games, and their actions played out badly as well.

Actions such as these have not typically resulted in statuary. Statues are typically erected to honor extraordinary persons and/or events. . . . It appears SJSU is attempting to start a new trend of statuary to honor those whose boorish behavior will not even rate a footnote to a footnote in the history books.

It is difficult to be horribly sarcastic in light of what you have done. . . . I just can't help myself. . . . I suppose the next statue at SJSU will be of Jane Fonda atop the anti-aircraft gun in Hanoi cheering the North Vietnamese soldiers.[59]

• • •

December 12, 2005

Dear Madam or Sir,

I received your Winter 2005 magazine in the mail and read about the statue you recently put on campus depicting an event that occurred at the Summer Olympics in Mexico.

I remember that Summer Olympics well because of the humiliation and sorrow I felt, as an American, at this inappropriate political gesture of militancy against my country on the world stage. That you would choose to immortalize this degrading moment in U.S. history is beyond comprehension!

If you think I am racially prejudiced, you think again. I myself am of mixed blood. My husband is a Jew who was enslaved (something these kids never suffered!) for five years in Hitler's slave labor camps, from age 13 to 17. The Rotary Club International brought him to the U.S.A. Every day he thanks America for giving him a home because he knows what real, not fictitious, oppression is! He came to America with $158.00 dollars in his pocket and became a useful citizen, a pediatrician, who not only put his four children through college, but several others also. Both he and I see the U.S.A. as truly a land of opportunity and personal freedom, not an oppressor as you, by immortalizing these young men displaying such bad judgment, seem to.

A University funded in part by our government should not use those funds to promote political hate and dissention. It is the job of a State University's leaders to take a dispassionate stand in politics and all other matters being inculcated into young minds. This you have failed to do by placing this obnoxious and offensive statue on San Jose State's campus. I suspect this badly thought out act to be the work of some aging left wing liberal hippies who have never succeeded in life and therefore find it easier to blame the system.

I have become very prosperous over the last decade. I was thinking of an endowment for San Jose State in my will. That will never happen now. Please remove my name from all your donor lists, as I no longer want it associated with San Jose State University.

Nevertheless, this sort of correspondence is merely one sign that this controversy is being revisited once again and in yet another cluttered fashion. For example, some, including the principal editors of the Black Athlete Sports Network, see the erection of this monument as a fitting commemoration of a watershed moment in American life with the potential for worldwide impact with the coming of the Beijing Olympics in 2008. They note:

While the grounds of San José State University might not compare with the Mall in Washington DC or Mount Rushmore as a place to be honored with a Statue it will do as well in cementing the importance of that Moment in American sports history.

In raising their fists covered by black gloves Smith and Carlos were inviting Wrath which they received in large measure, as their means of focusing on Racism in American society and to protest the Vietnam War as well. . . .

There is every reason to believe Smith's and Carlos' Black Fist Salute and specifically the photo which crystallizes it for all Eternity will live on and on, maybe even as much if not more many Generations from now . . . [a]nd serve as Inspiration and the Symbol for others who will seek to link the Olympics and repression or war in the most dramatic fashion.[60]

Others, however, were much less convinced of the implications of such a tribute, and while they may be no less supportive of Smith, Carlos, and their actions, they nonetheless look at this tribute as not an honor but rather as an insult to the memory and the legacy of the act itself and other acts of civil disobedience summarily suspended into popular culture. Dave Zirin, for instance, the author of the acclaimed *"What's My Name Fool?": Sports and Resistance in the United States,*[61] is decidedly aggrieved if not veritably unimpressed by it all. As he observes in an editorial written for the self-styled progressive *Common Dreams News Center:*

> Trepidation should be our first impulse when we hear that radical heroes are to be immortalized in fixed poses of bloodless nostalgia. There is something very wrong with seeing the toothy, grinning face of Paul Robeson staring back at us from a stamped envelope. Or the wry expression the US Postal service affixed on Malcolm X—harmless, wry, inviting, and by extension slanderous. . . . Those fears erupted when I heard that San José State University would be unveiling a statue of two of its alums, Tommie Smith and John Carlos. The 20 foot high structure would be a commemoration of their famed Black Gloved salute at the 1968 Olympics in Mexico City. I dreaded the thought that this would be the athletic equivalent to Lenin's Tomb: when you can't erase history, you simply embalm it.[62]

In this regard, as Zirin goes on to explain, turning this active challenge to the status quo into an inanimate hunk of material not only cheapens the memory but serves as well to demean the significance of struggle both then as now,[63] something Hartmann alludes to quite frequently in his pre-statue discussion of the legacy of the Mexico City protests.[64] Moreover, and as eloquently expressed by Professor Ethel Pitts-Walker during the dedication of the monument, the question of whether this relegates Smith and Carlos to an historical sideshow or is a call to arms for others to join the fray becomes the latest challenge to those upon whom she calls to "take up their activism and continue their work," something that Tommie Smith himself finds rather unrealistic given the temper of the times. As Elliott Almond of the *San José Mercury News* observed during a recent interview with Tommie Smith, Smith seems troubled by the more recent adulation concerning the statue and such. Moreover, while he is quick to note his appreciation for those who have stood by him throughout the long and at times humiliating road, he fears, among other matters, that his legacy will be solely framed within the "narrow prism of Mexico City,"[65] which so clearly misses the point of the entire episode. In other words, this may be exactly the sort of instance in which the icon of a truly iconic moment can look back and wonder—aloud or otherwise—whether his legacy will be little more than fodder for the very institutional machinery he had at one time hoped to rearrange, a fascinating (re)development indeed![66]

FINAL THOUGHTS

As if on cue, and within a month of the announcement of the forthcoming memorial sculpture, that same Smith and Carlos moment would scale the K2 of pop-cultural iconography when their likenesses appeared on *The Simpsons* episode entitled "My Mother the Carjacker." In this particular episode, the matriarchal Marge Simpson encourages her family to watch fictional KBBL news anchor Kent Brockman's "Oops Patrol," in which he shows what he terms a "stock montage" of historical events that some viewers might be "too young to remember."[67] Included amongst the significant images shown are those of former President Nixon's White House departure and his trademark "V," a symbol often used for "victory" and, as demonstrated by many Vietnam War protesters during the era, a gesture of peace, and what they too call Smith and Carlos's "Black Power" Salute.[68] Included on a Web discussion of this particular episode is a section called "Allusions" in which a fan of the show identifies Smith as an "American runner" before describing him as "giving the Black Panther salute in 1968." And still another fan, who appears as "chafear" on *The Simpsons*' Web site, refers to the protest in his review of the show as "that black pant(h)er thing."[69]

In all, this development, if one may call it that, was as predictable as it was admittedly irritating, though truth be told, there really is little to be done. Still, it does give one pause to consider Smith's above-noted comments regarding his and Carlos's legacy given these continued bouts of ill-conceived and certainly undignified misinformation. Nevertheless, or perhaps, more aptly, regardless of it all, in a most materially grounded sense, there really is little one can take from the controversy all these years later.

Perhaps the key to understanding the continuous loop of controversy combined with the unremitting stench of inaccuracy that this moment seems destined to attract can be found in the sustained reactions to the statue. On the other hand, that too may be mere folly. Either way, it is safe to assume, conceivably, that in some small corner of the world, someone is toying with the idea of protest but owning it as his or her own brand rather than merely mimicking something that has already been done. As John Carlos himself would note many years later, "I was representing shift workers, blue-collar people, the underdogs. That's why my shirt was open. Those are the people whose contributions to society are so important but don't get recognized."[70] After all, and at the end of the day, the point of all this was to shed light on those typically left outside the glow, and the image of the Avery Brundages, the J. Edgar Hoovers, the Brent Musburgers, and for that matter anyone else who might have reacted one way or the other really never was the issue, which of course begs the question: Why should it matter as such now?

NOTES

1. Yehuda Amichai, *Even a Fist Was Once an Open Palm with Fingers* (New York: Harper Perennial, 1991).

2. Ken Regan, *American Photographer*, 1996, p. 71.

3. Douglas Hartmann, *Race, Culture, and the Revolt of the Black Athlete: The 1968 Olympic Protests and Their Aftermath* (Chicago: University of Chicago Press, 2003), 9–10.

4. Hartmann, *Race, Culture*, 12.

5. Interestingly, RATM guitarist Tom Morello, whose father, Stephen Ngethe Njoroge, served as Kenya's first ambassador to the United Nations, actually had been nominated to receive the (John) Steinbeck Award for activism in 2005 from San José State University. That year, however, the honor was not awarded as Steinbeck's son, Thomas, was able to veto the nomination, as permitted by California civil code.

6. Rage Against the Machine, *Freedom Fighter of the Month*, http://www.ratm.com/new/freedom/main.html (12 January 2006).

7. Back Cover, *Black Men*, no. 65, August 2006.

8. Duncan MacKay, "Black Power Talking," *Athletics Weekly*, 55, no. 20. 16 May 2001: 23.

9. Hartmann, *Race, Culture*, 50.

10. The school was still known as Texas Western College when it won the 1965–66 NCAA men's basketball championship.

11. I should note here that San José State and UTEP did not schedule another contest until 1996, nearly thirty years after that history-making event. And Edwards would report that the cancellation of the contest cost both schools nearly $100,000. See Alan Tomlinson and Garry Whannel, *Five Ring Circus: Money, Power and Politics at the Olympic Games*, (London: Pluto Press, 1984), 40.

12. Urla Hill, "*Speed City*: The Civil Rights Years," (master's thesis, San Francisco State University, 2005), 40.

13. Harry Edwards, *The Revolt of the Black Athlete*, (New York: Free Press, 1970), 42.

14. No author, "A Declaration of Rights at San José," *San Francisco Chronicle*, 22 September 1967: 1A.

15. Hartmann, *Race, Culture*, 50.

16. Hartmann, *Race, Culture*, 50.

17. Hartmann, *Race, Culture*, 50.

18. Robert D. Clark, "Activism on Campus," *Peninsula Herald*, 19 October 1968: 65.

19. Edwards, *Revolt*, 43.

20. Jeffrey O. G. Ogbar, *Black Power: Radical Politics ad African American Identity* (Baltimore: Johns Hopkins University Press, 2004), 227.

21. Kevin B. Witherspoon, "Protest at the Pyramid: The 1968 Mexico City Olympics and the Politicization of the Olympic Games." PhD diss., Florida State University, 2003, 69.

22. Witherspoon, "Protest at the Pyramid," 41.

23. George Wright, interview by author, Chico, California, April 21, 2004. Wright is a retired political science professor from California State University at Chico.

24. Edwards, *Revolt*, 58–59.

25. Edwards, *Revolt*, 44.

26. No author, "Activism on Campus 1960s and 1970s," *Citizen News*, Hollywood, CA, 25 November 1967.

27. *Citizen News*.

28. An exhibit at the United States Holocaust Memorial Museum and titled "The Nazi Olympics: Berlin 1936," displays a proposal for a boycott of the 1936 Games.

29. Hartmann, *Race, Culture*, 64.

30. Edwards, *Revolt*, 58.

31. Gottfriend Korff, "From Brotherly Handshake to Militant Clenched Fist: On Political Metaphors for the Worker's Hand," *International Labor and Working-Class History*, no. 42 (Fall 1992): 71–72.

32. Phil Patton, "Not Your Grandparents' Clenched Fist," *Voice: AIGA Journal of Design*, 10 January 2006, http://voice.aiga.org/content.cfm?ContentAlias=_getfullarticle&aid=1402490 (21 April 2006).

33. Steven Hilliard Stern, *Fists of Freedom: The Story of the '68 Summer Games*, HBO Sports. Directed by George Roy (Black Canyon Productions, 1999).

34. George Willis, "2 Raised Fists Still Breaking Down Barriers," *New York Post On-Line*, 22 August 1999, http://promotions.nypost.com (22 August 2001).

35. Hartmann, *Race, Culture*, 174.

36. Martin Duberman, "Black Power and the American Radical Tradition," in *Left Out: The Politics of Exclusions/Essays 1964–1999*, ed. Martin Duberman (Cambridge, MA: South End Press, 2002), 169.

37. Duberman, "Black Power," 169.

38. Algernon Austin, "Cultural Black Nationalism and the Meaning of Black Power" (paper presented at the annual meeting of the American Sociological Association, Atlanta, GA, August 16, 2003). For more information, see Algernon Austin, *Achieving Blackness: Race, Black Nationalism, and Afrocentrism in the Twentieth Century* (New York: New York University Press, 2006).

39. Peniel E. Joseph, *Waiting 'til the Midnight Hour: A Narrative History of Black Power in America* (New York: Henry Holt and Co., 2006), xiv.

40. Joseph, *Waiting*, 174.

41. Edwards, *Revolt*, xv.

42. Edwards, *Revolt*, xv.

43. Jeffrey Ogbar, telephone interview by author, November 28, 2006. One film to which Ogbar refers is *La Bataille du Rail*. Réné Clément, Director/Writer. Coopérative Générale du Cinéma Français, 1946.

44. Kenny Moore, "A Courageous Stand: In '68, Olympians Tommie Smith and John Carlos Raised Their Fists for Racial Justice," *Sports Illustrated*, 5 August 1991, 72.

45. Ogbar, interview.

46. This seeming contradiction is not at all antithetical to a black American cultural legacy. In the African American tradition, badmen and heroes were often couched in the same heroic language if for no other reason than the badman's presence, one which did not placate but rather frightened mainstream whites, was considered to be a form of heroism in spite of the potential backlash this sort of behavior might bring. See, for example, Lawrence W. Levine, *Black Culture and Black Consciousness: Afro-American Folk Thought from Slavery to Freedom* (New York: Oxford University Press, 2007).

47. Martin Luther King, *Where Do We Go from Here: Chaos or Community* (New York: Harper & Row Publishers, 1967), 32.

48. Dick Hallgren, "San José Professor Joins Black Panthers," *San Francisco Chronicle*, 12 April 1968. San José State Special Collections. Folder: Racial Problems (general), Activism on Campus, 1960s and 1970s (Box 167, 168).

49. Hallgren, "San José Professor."

50. Hallgren, "San José Professor."

51. See, for example, Diaz, G. Pedro, "Victoria sin Violéncia en Mexico 68" (Victory without Violence in Mexico 68), *El Universal*, 21 October 2003: D1. Diaz reports that Smith remembers discussing

the pratfalls inherent to the Panther's platform with his teammates, noting that they agreed that they "didn't agree with the Black Panthers' tactics."

52. Robert D. Clark, "Wrath and Rapture in the Cult of Athletics," *San José Studies: San José State University Journal of Arts, Humanities, Social Sciences, and Business*, XIV, no. 3 (Fall 1988): 65.

53. Diaz, "Victoria sin Violéncia," D1.

54. Urla Hill, "The Protest of Champions: Looking Back on a Courageous Moment in Olympic History," *Dallas Morning News*, 19 September 1988: 1D. Oddly enough, and especially given his record on race, Cosell would describe the protest in his memoirs years later using the more pejorative language of black power. See, for example, Howard Cosell and Peter Bonventure, *I Never Played the Game* (New York: William Morrow, 1985).

55. Elliott Almond, "A Fist Frozen in Time: Tommie Smith Finally Tells Rest of the Story of His '68 Olympic Protest," *San José Mercury News*, 8 May 2007, http://www.mercurynews.com/books/ci_5831303 (26 June 2007).

56. Letter to San José State University. Please note that the names and addresses were removed by the university.

57. Letter to San José State University. Please note that the names and addresses were removed by the university.

58. This would be Gerald Selter, Executive Assistant to the President of San José State University.

59. Letter received by San José State University. Please note that the names and addresses were removed by the university.

60. No author, "Their Immortal Fists: Symbol of Defiance Will Now Live Forever (Maybe Even Send Message to China)," *Black Athlete Sports Network*, 30 May 2005. http://www.blackathlete.net/ Blackbox/blackbox053005.html, (27 June 2007). Note: All punctuation and capitalization printed verbatim from their original text.

61. Dave Zirin, *"What's My Name Fool?": Sports and Resistance in the United States*. (Chicago: Haymarket Books, 2005).

62. Dave Zirin, "When Fists Are Frozen: The Statue of Tommie Smith and John Carlos. *Common Dreams News Center*, 20 October 2005, http://www.commondreams.org/cgi-bin/print.cgi?file=/ views05/1020-28.htm (25 June 2007).

63. Zirin, "When Fists."

64. Hartmann, *Race, Culture*, 9–10.

65. Almond, "A Fist Frozen."

66. Tommie Smith and David Steele, *Silent Gesture: The Autobiography of Tommie Smith* (Philadelphia: Temple University Press, 2007).

67. *The Simpsons*, "My Mother the Carjacker," episode 315, March 1, 2007 (originally aired November 9, 2003).

68. *The Simpsons*, "My Mother."

69. *The Simpsons*, "My Mother."

70. Zirin, *What's My Name*, 88.

AFTERWORD

The Globalization of Vilification;
The Localization of Redemption

JACK LULE

In 476 B.C., in *Olympian Ode 1*, Pindar chronicled the disgrace of Tantalus. "If indeed the watchers of Olympus ever honored a mortal man, that man was Tantalus," Pindar wrote. But Tantalus, despite his great powers, prowess, and prosperity, lusted for more. He stole nectar and ambrosia from the gods and gave them to his drinking companions. Because of his greed, he earned overpowering ruin and a helpless life of never-ending labor. "If any man expects that what he does escapes the notice of a god, he is wrong," Pindar intoned.[1]

In summer 2007, as I write this, Barry Bonds, dogged for years by accusations of steroid use, has passed Hank Aaron as baseball's all-time home run leader. Michael Vick, quarterback of football's Atlanta Falcons, has been suspended for participating in illegal dog-fighting and is facing a prison term. Tim Donaghy, a veteran referee in the National Basketball Association, admitted to conspiring with gamblers to fix NBA games. Three riders, including the race leader, were thrown out of the Tour de France bicycle race for alleged steroid use.

"Sports' Worst Summer," or some variation thereof, the headlines read. But Pindar knew: stories of triumph and tragedy, honor and guilt, vilification and redemption will always be told. Indeed, years of research in history, folklore, anthropology, communication, history, religion, philosophy, and other fields have confirmed that mythic stories have existed as long as humans and may be integral to human existence.[2] Mircea Eliade, the historian of religion who studied myth in hundreds of societies, argued that aspects of mythical thought "are constituents of the human being." He wrote: "It seems unlikely that any society could completely dispense with myths, for, of what is essential in mythical behavior—the exemplary pattern, the repetition, the break with profane duration and integration into primordial time—the first two at least are consubstantial with every human condition."[3]

Sport has always been part of such mythic storytelling.[4] Founded upon drama, contest, and conflict, sport invokes the binary oppositions at the heart of myth—winning and losing, success and failure, life and death. Too, like myth, sport often is employed to celebrate, inculcate, and instill social values, such as sacrifice, courage, effort, teamwork, and perseverance. As Miller et al. (2001) state: "National mythmaking through sport is common as a means of generating new habits amongst the citizenry. Myths encourage active participation at the physical as well as the ideological level. Many accounts of sport situate it as a central tenet of national culture, in either a welcoming or a critical way. This reifies the term 'sport,' denying the social fissures—of gender, class, race, ethnicity, age, sexuality, media coverage, public participation, and region—that it engages."[5]

GLOBALIZATION AND SPORT

Though mythologizing about sport can be found throughout human history, modern myths of sport, I want to suggest, have assumed a distinctive, darker, more malevolent dimension in the late twentieth century and the new millennium. The forces of globalization, itself a contested term, have created renewed doubts about modernity, escalated tensions over racial, cultural, and ethnic identities, carved deep fissures along gender, labor, and class lines, and heightened levels of volatility and violence, all of which are continually revealed in myriad means of cultural production, including sport.

In one perspective, globalization may be as old as humankind's first steps away from the tribal campfire. Nayan Chanda, who directs Yale's globalization project, finds that globalization has stemmed from a basic human urge to seek a better life and has been driven by numerous actors throughout history, including traders, preachers, adventurers, and warriors. Chanda says, "The term *globalization*, reflecting awareness of these global connections, grew out of the very process it describes—a process that has worked silently for millennia without having been given a name."[6]

Though accepting that globalization has precursors and precedents centuries old, other scholars argue that globalization is decidedly a phenomenon of modernity. Cultural anthropologist Arjun Appadurai finds that the twentieth century experienced "a rupture" in which modern media technology and mass migration combined in exceptional ways that provided new resources for the imagination—the construction of imagined selves and imagined worlds. "This mobile and unforeseeable relationship between mass-mediated events and migratory audiences" Appadurai writes, "defines the core of the link between globalization and the modern."[7]

Whether conceived as a centuries-old phenomenon or modern rupture, globalization undoubtedly shapes and is shaped by sport, which is central to social life. The multivalent relationship between globalization and sport can be identified and approached in numerous ways. Surely, the professionalization of modern sport,[8] the commodification of sport,[9] global marketing and promotion,[10] the political economy of sport media,[11] global sport and cultural labor,[12] and the globalization of events from the Olympics to the World Cup offer invaluable subjects of study.

Of particular interest, however, especially to this volume, is the social uncertainty spawned by the amalgam of globalization and sport, and the myriad attempts to mitigate, repair, and resolve that uncertainty.

THE GLOBALIZATION OF VILIFICATION

Through sport and throughout sport, social uncertainty raised by globalizing forces has played out on ballfields, locker rooms, and bleachers, as well as kitchen tables and living rooms. Forces of globalization—which include the professionalization and division of labor, the expansion of global marketing and commodification of celebrities, mass migration and diaspora, and the relentless global economy—brought vast changes in race, class, gender, and wealth to sport in the last fifty years. Chronicled by newspapers, magazines, radio broadcasts, television programs, films, and the Internet, these changes agitate populaces, who often seek in sport a distraction from the world's cares and concerns.

As this volume has shown, sport figures who, willingly or unwillingly, come to represent social change and uncertainty, especially in the arena of race, find themselves victims of degradation and deprecation. The fates of individual players rise, fall, and rise again not often from their own actions but from the waves of social uncertainty roiling their societies and times. Jackie Robinson, descendant of slaves forcibly emigrated to America, stepped onto the professional baseball fields of white men, in the dawning of the civil rights era, and set off social shockwaves that still resound today. Roberto Clemente came to the Unites States from Puerto Rico, embodying the large influx of Latinos populating America, and sport audiences responded with a combustible mixture of worship and hatred, desire and degradation.

These impulses, acted out through the twentieth century, continue to have especial relevance in our own times of immigration debates, civil war, religious fundamentalism, and ethnic cleansing. Appadurai notes that such social uncertainty cuts to the very heart of identity for individuals and groups: "This species of uncertainty is intimately connected to the reality that today's ethnic groups number in the hundreds of thousands and that their movements, mixtures, cultural styles, and media representations create profound doubts about who exactly are among the 'we' and who are among the 'they.'"[13]

The destruction and reconstruction of sport figures in the name of social uncertainty can also be understood in mythic terms. Social groups often find resolution of "we" versus "they" tensions through enactments of the scapegoat ritual. In this ritual, the uncertainties, doubts, misfortunes, or faults of a society are symbolically "loaded upon" an individual or group. With the assignation of blame, attempts are then made to symbolically drive out or cast out the scapegoat from society. Sir

James George Frazer saw these rituals as "public attempts to expel the accumulated ills of a whole community."[14] The scapegoat ritual assigns and isolates blame—and relieves social uncertainty—by banishing the blameworthy from the social circle.

The scapegoat ritual has taken on horrific proportions in modern societies. In a most extreme form, Nazis used the Jews as scapegoats for ills besetting German society. The 1994 Rwandan genocide saw the mass killing of hundreds of thousands of ethnic Tutsis by extremist Hutu militia groups. Less extreme examples can be found throughout modern times. African Americans have been deemed responsible for urban crime and drug use. Illegal immigrants have been deemed responsible for U.S. unemployment. Working women have been deemed responsible for the breakup of families. Scapegoats are seemingly always available for social ills.

In times of social uncertainty, sport heroes have proven to be particularly adaptable subjects for the scapegoat ritual. They are recognizable with international celebrity status, but are largely unknown as real people, and thus their reputations—their stories—are highly malleable. Muhammad Ali, for example, was an apt scapegoat in the 1960s, embodying American fears over black power, urban violence, protest over the war in Vietnam, tensions between young and old, and other social anxieties. John Carlos and Tommie Smith, known only as successful Olympic track stars to many Americans in 1968, immediately embodied fears over racial tensions and black power by raising their fists in symbolic protest on the medals stand.

The resulting scapegoat rituals can prove savage; cultural forces can respond with fury to confusion and uncertainty. Ali was stripped of his title and sentenced to jail. Carlos and Smith were suspended from their national team and banned from the Olympic Village, while they and their families were the subjects of death threats. As scapegoats, these sport stars were loaded with the huge weight of social uncertainty and fear, assigned blame, and driven from the social circle.

THE LOCALIZATION OF REDEMPTION

As writers in this volume have emphasized, it is striking how often the vilified sport hero has found redemption in modern mythologizing. Ali, shaking and debilitated from Parkinson's disease, was chosen to light the flame at the 1996 Olympics in Atlanta. Carlos and Smith, now coaches for high school track teams, were honored in ceremonies throughout 1998, the thirtieth anniversary of their protest. Seemingly, the scapegoats of globalization and vilification can find redemption.

However, it is important to note that the ritual of redemption often is only the final act in the drama of vilification. In the first acts, the sport hero serves as a scapegoat who embodies the sins and doubts of society; the scapegoat is degraded and demeaned and driven out of the social circle. The redemption of the sport hero occurs only when social uncertainty eases and when the hero no longer represents a threat to social order. Then, the once-disgraced sport hero is permitted, literally or symbolically, back into society, no longer outcast, no longer foreign, the localization of redemption.

It is also important to note: the vilified sports hero does not *achieve* redemption but is *granted* redemption. Myth and ritual are always tied to social order. Just as the scapegoat ritual unfolds to repair social order, the accompanying ritual of redemption unfolds to confirm the repair and to affirm the rightness and righteousness of social order. For example, Pete Rose, denied entry into baseball's Hall of Fame for betting on the game, has yet to be redeemed. Barry Bonds, having set the all-time home run figure this summer but shadowed by allegations of steroid use, remains outside the social pale. Sport heroes are redeemed when they can advance and confirm social order. When they cannot, they remain, like Tantalus, helplessly outside the social circle, wandering far from the joy of festivity.

CONCLUSION

Globalization undoubtedly has given rise to social uncertainty in economics, politics, culture, and other walks of life. Because of its central role in social life, sport has been a significant arena in which social uncertainties spawned by globalization have played out. Globalizing forces, from the commodification of athletes to mass migration and diaspora, have yielded vast changes in sport. For those who were not at the ballparks, the continuously evolving media have brought home the unsettling social scene.

Such soaring social uncertainty, especially surrounding the flashpoint of race, brings with it the savage solace of the scapegoat ritual as societies seek to resolve uncertainty by blaming an "other." Globalization has accelerated, diversified, and intensified the rituals of degradation in sport, particularly those invoking race, providing more subjects and more opportunities for absorbing cultural dramas of vilification.

As Pindar has shown, the stakes can be high. Rituals of degradation surrounding sport can lead to outbreaks of violence and lifetimes of exclusion. Yet it is humbling and frightening to consider that sport offers only microcosms of scapegoat rituals, which can grow to encompass ethnocide and genocide. At times, one can only hope, with Pindar, that, "If any man expects that what he does escapes the notice of a god, he is wrong."[15]

NOTES

1. Pindar, *The Ode.* (New York: Penguin Books, 1982). Translation from C. M. Bowra (8 August 2007) http://www.perseus.tufts.edu/cgibin/ptext?doc=Perseus%3Atext%3A1999.01.0162.

2. Jack Lule, *Daily News, Eternal Stories: The Mythological Role of Journalism* (New York: Guilford, 2001), 1–38.

3. Mircea Eliade, *Myths, Dreams and Mysteries*, Philip Mairet, trans. (New York: Harper & Brothers, 1960), 31–32.

4. Peter Williams, *The Sports Immortals: Deifying the American Athlete* (Bowling Green, OH: Bowling Green State University Press, 1994), 39–62.

5. Toby Miller, Geoffrey Lawrence, Jim McKay, and David Rowe, *Globalization and Sport: Playing the World* (Thousand Oaks, CA: Sage, 2001), 3.

6. Nayan Chanda, *Bound Together: How Traders, Preachers, Adventurers, and Warriors Shaped Globalization* (New Haven: Yale University Press, 2007), xi.

7. Appaurai continues, "Thus, to put it summarily, electronic mediation and mass migration mark the world of the present not as technically new forces but as ones that seem to impel (and sometimes compel) the work of the imagination." In Arjun Appadurai, *Modernity at Large: Cultural Dimensions of Globalization* (Minneapolis: Public Worlds and University of Minnesota Press, 1996), 4.

8. See Barry Smart, *The Sport Star: Modern Sport and the Cultural Economy of Sporting Celebrity* (Thousands Oaks, CA: Sage, 2005).

9. See Michael Real, "MediaSport: Technology and the Commodification of Postmodern Sport," in *MediaSport*, ed. Lawrence Wenner (London: Routledge, 1998), 14–26.

10. See David Whitson, "Circuits of Promotion: Media, Marketing and the Globalization of Sport," in *MediaSport*, ed. Lawrence Wenner (London: Routledge, 1998), 57–72.

11. See David Rowe, *Sport, Culture and the Media* (Buckingham, England: Open University Press, 1999).

12. See Miller, *Globalization and Sport.*

13. Arjun Appadurai, *Fear of Small Numbers: An Essay on the Geography of Anger* (Durham, NC: Duke University Press, 2006), 5.

14. Sir James George Frazer, *The Golden Bough, Vol. 9: The Scapegoat* (New York: Macmillan, 1951), 109.

15. Pindar, *The Odes.*

CONTRIBUTORS

PROSPER GODONOO is director of the Paul Robeson Cultural Center at Rutgers where he also teaches courses within the Department of Africana Studies. He has taught at the college and secondary school levels in Canada, Ghana, and Nigeria for twenty years; has had extensive experience in African outreach activities in UCLA, University of Illinois, and Rutgers: and has conducted many workshops on teaching about Africa. He has also developed curriculum units about the continent for American educators.

URLA HILL left her career as a sportswriter to return to her alma mater, San José State University, to study the black athletic experience on campus during the civil rights and black power movements. The native Californian currently is working toward a Ph.D. in American studies at the University of Maryland. She also is working with History San José on an exhibit and documentary to be based on her thesis, "*Speed City: The Civil Rights Years.*"

C. RICHARD KING, associate professor of comparative ethnic studies at Washington State University, has written extensively on the changing contours of race in post–civil rights America, the colonial legacies and postcolonial predicaments of American culture, and struggles over Indianness in public culture. His work has appeared in a variety of journals, such as *American Indian Culture and Research Journal, Journal of Sport and Social Issues, Public Historian,* and *Qualitative Inquiry.* He is also the author/editor of several books, including *Team Spirits: The Native American Mascots Controversy* (a CHOICE 2001 Outstanding Academic Title) and *Postcolonial America.* He has recently completed *Visual Economies in/of Motion: Sport and Film.*

DAVID J. LEONARD is assistant professor in the Department of Comparative Ethnic Studies at Washington State University. His work focuses on sports, video games, and film, appearing in both popular and academic mediums. He recently published, with C. Richard King, *Visual Economies in/of Motion: Sport and Film*, an edited volume on sports films, and a monograph, *Screen Fade to Black: Contemporary African Cinema.* He is currently working on a monograph looking at race and the culture wars of the NBA and another (with C. Richard King) analyzing the production and consumption of media culture within white nationalist communities.

JACK LULE is the Joseph B. McFadden Professor in Journalism in the Department of Journalism and Communication at Lehigh University. His research interests include cultural and critical studies of news, international communication, online journalism, sports and media, and teaching with technology. He is the author of more than thirty-five scholarly articles and book chapters, is a member of the editorial board of *Journalism and Mass Communication Quarterly*, and is associate editor of *Critical Studies in Media Communication*.

MURRY NELSON is professor of education and American studies at Pennsylvania State University where he received the first President's Award for Excellence in Academic Integration (1997). He has been a Fulbright Senior Scholar at the University of Iceland (1983) and with the Norwegian Ministry of Education, Religion and Research (1990–91) and has written numerous articles, chapters, and books on a wide range of subjects including a biography of Bill Russell published in 2005.

DAVID C. OGDEN is associate professor of communications at the University of Nebraska at Omaha. He has taught at UNO since 2001, and was associate professor at Wayne State College in Nebraska prior to his current appointment. His research focuses on cultural trends in baseball, specifically the history of the relationship between African Americans and baseball. He has presented his research at the National Baseball Hall of Fame Symposium on Baseball and American Culture, the *Nine* Spring Training Conference on Baseball and Culture, and Indiana State University's Conference on Baseball in Culture and Literature. He has published in *NINE: A Journal of Baseball History & Culture*, the *Journal of Leisure Research*, and the *Journal of Black Studies*.

ROBERT W. REISING is professor in education at the University of the Cumberlands in Williamsburg, Kentucky. Prior to that he spent nearly thirty years as jointly a professor in the English Department as well as the Department of Native American Literature at University of North Carolina–Pembroke. From fall 2003 through fall 2004, he served as a visiting scholar in the American Indian Studies program at Michigan State University. He is currently working on his third book on Native American athlete Jim Thorpe.

JOEL NATHAN ROSEN is assistant professor of sociology at Moravian College in Bethlehem, Pennsylvania. He is the author of *The Erosion of the American Sporting Ethos: Shifting Attitudes Toward Competition* (McFarland 2007) and has been published in various journals and periodicals including *Media History Monographs*, the *Journal of Mundane Behavior*, *NINE: A Journal of Baseball History & Culture*, and *Living Blues Magazine*.

INDEX